Hope is a Verb

A woman's journey from hopelessness to
learning to live fully with chronic depression

THERESA A. CATANIA

I dedicate this book to Dr. Philip M. Drucker for helping me discover a flower blooming in the nethermost depth of my darkness. This book, along with the awakening of hope, is only possible because of his support.

ACKNOWLEDGEMENTS

Above all, I would like to express my deepest gratitude to Dr. Philip M. Drucker, Associate Professor of Psychology at St. John's University and author of Hope Road, for providing encouragement and support through the long and difficult writing journey and for assisting in the editing and proofreading of this book. Mostly, I would like to thank him for showing me that "*hope can work.*"

I would like to express my appreciation to my brother Louis who supported me through hurdles during the writing of this book. His assistance helped me to stay focused on meaningful work despite my challenges.

I would like to thank Dr. Patrick Williams, author, speaker, Life and Wellness Coach, for accepting my invitation to read the final draft of my book and for generously offering to contribute the Foreword. I would also like to thank Dr. Pat for encouraging me to be vulnerable and expose my naked truth.

Thank you Maria Jürimäe for the cover illustration.

Thank you Krissy Carstens, KrissArt Marketing Design, for the title page illustration.

I would like to thank Christine Fede Williams for providing inspiration and advice.

I would like to thank all of the teachers, writers, philosophers and poets who came before me and inspired the writing of my story.

Finally, I would like to acknowledge my kindred spirits who live with depression and anxiety. It is because of you that I wrote these words.

FOREWORD

First of all, let me say I am honored to write this foreword to **Hope is a Verb**, a book written with such honesty and insight that it can be extremely helpful to those who are challenged with depression or anxiety or other effects from living on the edge of life's many challenges and journeys and unexpected side trips.

Theresa has compiled a book that is a narrative from the heart and soul written as a personal journey in and out of depression and a personal road map of how she continued to rise. As she says in the final chapter,

"Each small step that you take today will lead to a more purposeful and hopeful tomorrow. Hope is a verb. "

In my book, **Getting Naked: On Emotional Transparency at the Right Time, the Right Place, and with the Right Person**, I write that every experience can be a good experience eventually. We experience both chosen and unchosen change. But even if we experience what we would not have chosen; we eventually have to make a choice in how to respond, and accept *what is* and learn from it so we can move from *what was* to *what will be*. And sharing these times in real conversation with a trusted listener is what getting emotionally naked is really about. Live purposefully, never perfectly.

Life is continuously providing us information or messages. When we do not listen, the messages become lessons. When we do not learn, the lessons become problems. When we don't address the problems, they become crises. When crises go unresolved, they create chaos in our lives.

Great students of life seek to live on the levels of messages and lessons, not waiting for them to become problems, crises, and chaos. Keeping life's processes on the lesson and message level makes living so much more enjoyable. As is often said, no matter how hard we plan, life happens. It's what we do with it and how we respond that matters most. Having someone to share your naked truth with is crucial to your resilience. Being witnessed makes you feel held, which in turn makes you more receptive to life's bigger purpose. From there, you can become more capable to reawaken your awareness of your own inner identity, to discover your personal/professional vision and purpose, and to sharpen communication with yourself and others. The ultimate result is being able to live in such an intentional manner that who you are as a person becomes the catalyst for a fulfilling experience of this precious time on earth.

Self-protection is a very human instinct, one at which we are universally proficient. We have all learned to wear masks and protective armor from a young age and rightfully so. The world is not a place to be vulnerable all the time. Self-control defends us against intimacy, letting us track the parameters in order to avoid being absorbed into the spaciousness that resides within.

Theresa has written an extremely poignant and self-revealing book that shares her story of struggle with depression in and out of the many ages and stages of her life. And yet, the lesson herein, is one that deeply touched me and also pointed to a ray of light for others in a similar life struggle. As a psychologist of 20 years, and a Life and Wellness Coach for even more now, I read with awe the poetic beauty of Theresa's narrative, her life story, written and expressed with such honesty and emotional nakedness.

Courageous sharing with a committed and trusted listener is how we break out of our self-imposed prison.

The magic of revealing ourselves to a trusted other allows us to reclaim energy that has been keeping the cellar door locked. (From **Getting Naked** by Patrick Williams)

From standing on the edge of the Golden Gate Bridge contemplating suicide, Theresa has chosen a leap of faith instead.

Theresa has shared with you her story.... what is your story and with whom can you share it? In doing so you will be reclaiming parts of your SELF that have been locked away due to shame, guilt, fear, or even dreams that you gave up on because no one encouraged their expression.

Take Theresa's narrative and her message of hope to heart. You have nothing to lose and everything to gain. Live your life beyond mediocrity and beyond just settling for survival. Instead, this book will move you to live with purpose, and courage, and hope! Hope IS a verb. And a verb implies action. As professional coaches, we listen to our clients and help them say what they have not said, hear what they have not heard, and to dream out loud with a trusted listener. Let Theresa be your coach through her story. And allow her insights to be your guide to action. Then find your trusted listener and share your naked truth, not to fix anything...just to reveal and reclaim who you are meant to be

Dr. Patrick Williams
Author, Speaker, Life and Wellness Coach
Author of *Getting Naked: On Emotional Transparency at the Right Time, the Right Place, and with the Right Person.*

INTRODUCTION

As I peered over the railing with my new husband on a particularly crisp September morning, I imagined the strong currents beneath the bridge welcoming me and washing me out to sea. I gazed at the serene early autumn blue skies against the magnificent California hills and understood, with a new-found visceral intensity, why this landmark attracts individuals contemplating suicide. Perhaps, I thought, destiny has brought me to the Golden Gate Bridge at this precise moment in my life. If I climbed over the low railing all of my pain would be over in just a few seconds and I would be in total control of my fate. But instead I left my heart at the Golden Gate Bridge and walked away.

It's been over two decades since I stood at the threshold of life and death. This was the watershed moment which divided my personal history into two distinct parts: my earlier life leading up to the Golden Gate Bridge when my depressive illness was not entirely manifested and my life following the Golden Gate Bridge when it seemed as if the earth changed its rotational direction as I plunged into an internal ocean of mental illness.

My name is Blank and I am a middle aged woman who suffers from treatment-resistant chronic depression, a term used for individuals with a major depressive disorder whose symptoms have not been relieved after numerous antidepressant trials. My treatment-resistant depression along with the stigma and abiding loneliness that ensued is the reality I have come to know. I encapsulated my personal history here in a collection of essays that tell the story of my life so that you will understand the insipid and gradual nature of depression. Most importantly, if you come along with me on this journey, you will discover that even if your struggles are chronic in nature - it is possible to experience the familiar heartbeat of hope again.

At first I wasn't drawn to writing about what appeared to be an unremarkable childhood, however, after feverishly writing pages and pages of practical and profoundly emotional content on my experiences since the Golden Gate Bridge, I realized that the content did not begin to explore a fundamental question: Where did all the emotional pain come from? Assembling the relevant moments of my childhood was difficult because I was forced to confront – repeatedly - the paralyzing juxtaposition of all that I could have been with the person that I have become today.

It wasn't until I finished the first draft of my book and mentally took a step back that I was able to see my life in its entirety. I learned that objects and experiences are not completely visible unless you take some time to step away and observe them from a distance. The need to share my larger perspective was tugging at my heart so I decided to go back to the beginning and add the *Reflections* that you will find at the end of each chapter. In a sense, my book went through two phases of deep reflection: the earlier phase presented a detailed emotional account of my life experiences and the later phase offered a renewed perspective that gives clarity and meaning to my narrative.

I am committed to telling my version of the truth with as much openness and honesty as possible, however, in several instances I changed names to protect the privacy of the individuals that are involved in my life story. I decided to use the pseudonym, Blank, because it provided some emotional distance when critical self-judgment became a major obstacle during the writing process. By incorporating this technique I found that I was able to thrust myself into the deepest parts of my psyche while alleviating some of the negativity. I also assigned the analogous name, Blank2, to my therapist because I think of him as an extension of myself, a routine participant in my internal and external communication. Once the book was completed it was my intention to replace the pseudonyms with proper names, but I was unable to say goodbye to Blank and Blank2. In the name Blank I found a place to be free from judgment, an alternate identity where it was acceptable to speak openly about my depression. The name Blank became like a blank canvas where I was free to paint my most pure self using shades of darkness and light. A painter has an appreciation for the blank canvas and a writer, I learned, treasures the creative freedom of a blank page.

One of the prevailing characteristics of this book is that many of the chapters focus on specific subject matters, such as my belief system, bullying, a family holiday tradition, and therapy. I use comprehensive flashbacks and flash forwards within each chapter taking you with me on a heartfelt and emotional journey of self discovery and acceptance. Hopefully, by the end of my book you will be left with a broad view of chronic major depression as described with raw lucidity in my voice. What separates my book from other works on depression is that, as a chronic depressive, it had to be written in the midst of the disease instead of during periods of remission or recovery. This revelation is critical because it bears a vital message: there is hope in despair and it can be found in the strength and determination of those who struggle.

Before writing I believed that my life was consumed by the flames of depression, like a brush fire consumes a forest, leaving it barren of all its potential beauty; however as my writing progressed I discovered the hidden beauty of adversity in the invaluable lessons that I learned along the way. Hidden deep inside of my broken spirit I found a purpose, a reason for my existence - and I want to inspire you to find the light in the darkness too.

Part One

FORESHADOWING

Chapter One

HOME

I am a depressive. When I finally said those words to myself, it was already too late. In my early years I drifted heedlessly along a precarious path, like a leaf swirling acquiescently in the bleak autumn wind. How could I fully grasp the unpleasant "D" word when my family was habitually stuck in a denial stage of my mother's advancing symptoms of multiple sclerosis and bouts of depression? My mother's illness was hidden behind an inexhaustible mask of excuses until we were forced to submit to the strong will of her progressive disease. I never thought about how my home environment and genes came together to shape my own demons until I found myself inside the closed world of a psychiatric hospital in my late twenties.

As a child I did think about how my family seemed slightly flawed, especially set against the backdrop of the immutable perfection of our Staten Island neighborhood. Our home was situated in a high elevation valley just yards away from the base of a majestic hill. The hill formed a natural protective barrier between our neighborhood and the outside world while echoing the sounds of unconstrained laughter of the many children that lived in the community. The hills were so steep and difficult to navigate by foot or bicycle that my brother and I remained with an awkward upward strut as adults.

I had a strange ache inside of me whenever I looked at the treeless suburban streets until the day the community voted to plant trees alongside the curbs and little by little the juvenile trees brought color and charm to our neighborhood. I was probably no more than six years old when I was told that the trees would one day grow quite tall and wide, however, it was difficult for me to imagine the passage of time and the maturation of all living things back then. Nevertheless, the trees taught me to look forward to tomorrow. My neighbors had planted the seeds of hope.

The views from my childhood home were brilliant. During the day we could see the surrounding hill from almost any window. Rumor had it that Native American Indians lived on reservations in the hill and I spent much of my childhood searching for evidence. At times I thought I could hear the echo of their spiritual chanting and the beating of their drums. At night the Verrazano Bridge flaunted its beauty through my bedroom window with its delicate strands of lights that formed a glittering necklace which connected Staten Island to Brooklyn. I was filled with pride each time my father mentioned that he owned the twinkling lights that adorned the bridges two towers, however, I later realized that it was his creative way of expressing his frustration over paying the high tolls necessary to exit the borough.

My parents were of modest means, but as a child I was under the impression that we were poor because I often made comparisons with the more well-to-do families that sported a Cadillac or Mercedes in their driveway. My father considered the Cadillac to be a hallmark of American quality and excellence; and as a result of this belief he tended to compare his most prized possessions to the luxury vehicle. I would often hear him say things like, "this is the Cadillac of cameras" or "this is the Cadillac of sound systems." One day my father purchased a new Buick and announced to my mother that "this is the Cadillac of all cars." My mother responded with a soft laugh, half serious and half in jest, "sweetheart, why didn't you just buy the Cadillac?" He never used the Cadillac analogy again.

The neighborhood was the home of a diverse group which included a variety of mundane folks and also some unordinary folks like the woman who suffered from a severe form of schizophrenia and another neighbor who was part of an organized crime family. The neighborhood adults were not the friendly variety that generously invited children into their homes and lives, but I always felt a sense of trust and security when they were around. Looking back, I consider my childhood neighborhood to be an idyllic place to grow up. I'm even nostalgic about some of my unfavorable experiences, like the time I was injured when my bicycle lost its brakes and I barreled down the steep road until I finally slammed into a tree. These good and bad memories will always be powerfully meaningful to me because the old neighborhood is the foundation of my life narrative.

My best friend and I were Americans of Italian descent, but our features were strikingly dissimilar. Donna had a sturdy physique, rosy complexion, flaxen hair, and soft azure eyes; whereas I was gaunt with intense dark features and a sallow skin tone. We shared a magical friendship, always living in the moment with unsuppressed energy. I recall the excitement of being invited into Donna's home at the age of six to watch The Wizard of Oz shown in amazing *Technicolor*. From then on viewing this showing became our cherished annual tradition. Since Donna's mother was a working woman and my mother ill, we were incredibly independent children. Our unbridled days were filled with wonderment whether we just stayed on our street and played hopscotch or explored the deep hills in search of rock diamonds and Native American Indians. I shudder to think that we were innocent children adventuring through the desolate hill without fear, but, when Donna was around I never feared much of anything. Donna was my sense of normalcy in a childhood with increasing struggles and I found strength in our friendship.

My older brother's cheery personality was treasured by our family and neighbors. Unlike me, he was the kind of kid who would wake up and go to sleep with a smile on his face. My brother and his best buddy, Lenny, spent endless hours just hanging out or playing softball on our quiet streets into the late evenings, and each Halloween they would trick or treat with the enthusiasm of jewel thieves after a successful heist. As teenagers in the late 1970's they often reflected on pro-rock or pro-disco sentiments. Back then many of our neighborhood teens were divided by preferences in music genres and not by class or religion.

The day I graduated from high school marked the period of time when I began to realize that my life was dramatically changing and things would never be the same again. I looked into the audience of the High School's quaint chapel and was unable to find my parents. My mother's disease was becoming increasingly aggressive and diminished her quality of life and consequently the quality of life of our family and sometimes it was difficult to share milestone events.

In addition, Donna moved away from the neighborhood not long after our graduation and eventually settled in another state and my brother and Lenny were also emerging from the neighborhood cocoon. Day by day I was experiencing an elusive misery that seemed to run deep inside the marrow of my bones; a feeling more chilling than loneliness because I believed that no one could save me from my profound sense of powerlessness and isolation.

During this period I recall looking at the changing landscape outside my front window while the weight of my sadness was dragging me down. It struck me how the young trees seemed to suddenly mature, spreading their limbs expansively throughout the neighborhood. My new perception of nature created feelings of fear relating to the loss of control over time. I was beginning to conceptualize the changing of the winds through the lens of a depressive, even though I still could not define my enveloping mood disorder.

These days I fantasize about going back in time to the only place that I would know a sense of community. I never imagined then that I would eventually end up on the other side of the hill alone and in a small flat situated in a densely populated area where no one knows my name. Perhaps if I close my eyes and tap my heels three times while repeating: "There's no place like home," I will awake in my childhood abode with family and friends around me – after all it worked for Dorothy in the Wizard of Oz.

Reflections on Chapter 1: Home

When I first wrote this chapter it was nothing more than an isolated exercise in creative writing, but Blank2 immediately understood its potential and it soon became the inspiration for writing a book. Metaphorically speaking, "Home" unintentionally became one of the main themes in my book since, in later chapters, I wrote obsessively about isolation and yearnings to find my way back to a place where I felt safe and loved.

As a child I took my landscape for granted, never realizing that each and every experience contributed to a larger meaning. In actuality, the home that I grew up in was the physical space that supported my growth and shaped who I am today.

Walking through a portal to my childhood home gave me hope that my depression could be alleviated by increasing my understanding of the environment where my emotional pain began; and, conversely, by reconnecting to the happiness I experienced in my youth. As a result of my depression, I have looked at the world through dark-colored glasses for so many years that it is difficult for me to remember what happiness feels like, but writing about my childhood home helped me to remember and gave me hope that maybe one day I could feel happiness again. As Dorothy might say if she were here today: "There's no place like HOPE."

Chapter Two

BELIEVE

I was a six year old first grader enmeshed in darkness the first time I pondered the mystery of my Roman Catholic faith. I am referring to the stark darkness of Sister Stella's religious habit and not the darkness of despair that I would eventually come to know.

"Blank, bend over my knees so that I could paddle you for not completing your homework assignment."

"Yes, Sister."

Sister Stella's long black veil exposed a limited view of her stern and determined face. As I rested over Sister Stella's knees I observed her unconstrained holy habit which was made of heavy black fabric that draped to the ground. Belts and cords gathered her tunic at the waist where rosary beads hung. I could see Sister Stella's hands clenching the paddle through her long flowing sleeves but I did not fear my impending punishment because I was distracted by a feverish curiosity over the obscurity of Sister Stella's vestment. I was compelled to run my hands through the abundant layers of her habit because I believed that somewhere hidden deep within the underskirts, overskirts, aprons, belts, and rosary beads - the mystery of God would be revealed.

For the next fourteen years I embarked upon my religious education as a student in the Catholic school system, a parishioner of the Catholic Church and a student at a Catholic university. I learned that the Church is the vessel of the teachings of Christ as well as the Bible. I became familiar with Catholic prayers, songs of worship, images and genuflection. I revered the blessed mother Mary and all of the saints. I attempted to accept that the Eucharist is literally the body and blood of Christ and not a symbol and I believed in the unfathomable mystery of the Trinity.

Finally, I received all of the relevant sacraments and despite my unshakable apprehension I routinely participated in the Sacrament of Penance to confess my sins. In an effort to save my soul from eternal damnation I routinely entered a dark confessional box shrouded in mystery as a priest sat in a separate compartment behind a lattice.

"Bless me Father for I have sinned."

"Tell me your sins my child."

"I do not honor my mother and father at all times. I'm defiant and temperamental. I missed mass on a Holy Day of Obligation. That's all my sins for now Father."

"Please recite the act of contrition."

"O my God, I am heartily sorry for all my sins, because they offend You, who are infinitely good, and I firmly resolve with the help of thy grace to sin no more and to avoid the near occasion of sin."

"Through the power of the Holy Spirit your sins are forgiven."

"Thank you, Father."

Over and over again I quietly rose from the kneeler and walked away from the confessional free from sin - but not free from guilt; and fulfilled because I had completed my commitment to the sacrament – but not spiritually fulfilled. I whispered my sins to the priest while longing to break the confessional protocol and utter the words:

'Father, please step away from behind the lattice and look into my eyes to see that I am also a victim of sin and suffering. I endure excessive bullying at school, I fear evil and lay awake at nights, my mother is very ill, I do not feel a sense of community in the Church - please help me Father before it's too late to save my soul.'

As a child I held all the sacraments and beliefs of the Roman Catholic Church as true without question much in the same way that I believed in Santa Claus. So I believed in God – though I never felt His presence. However, as I moved through life I began to challenge the Christian concepts of evil and suffering and found it difficult to accept that a loving and all-knowing God would permit the depravity of humanity.

I began to ask questions like if man has free will, as Catholics believe, how could God be all-knowing? Does God deliver suffering so that we may turn to Him for divine grace? I personally attest to the many occasions when I have fallen on my knees begging for His mercy asking, as Jesus asked in the final moments of his crucifixion, "My God, my God, why have you forsaken me?" Yet over and over again I did not find a recognizable divine grace.

I am willing to postulate that evil and suffering benefit humanity in ways that are not always understood in the moment.

History informs us that evil brought Jesus to the cross and consequently His suffering and death was the catalyst to a major religion which has bestowed care to the sick and education and social services throughout the world.

But what about those who suffer and do not have the ability to contribute to our humanity like my mother who spent a lifetime suffering from disease? One can always argue that their suffering could ultimately teach valuable lessons on faith, hope and love. Although this is a redeeming quality of suffering, I don't believe that it justifies sacrificing the life and well-being of the innocent.

I am beginning to understand that my own struggles have given me the insight to help those in despair and perhaps contribute, in some small way, to the greater good, although I never asked for adversity. Instead, as a child I prayed for a mother to be well but her disease grew rampant; I prayed for friendships among schoolmates and received unbearable mockery; I prayed to be nurtured and cared for and instead became a caretaker. And, as an adult I prayed for friends and a family of my own but instead I am alone; I prayed for men who could love me but became a victim of cruelty; I prayed to be less sensitive to the world around me, but instead I experience a heightened sensitivity to almost everything and everyone; and I prayed for strength but I am weak. Most importantly, through all my despair, I prayed to feel a connection to God and my community of worshipers - yet I felt nothing but emptiness. I probably would have maintained my faith despite unanswered prayers and the complexity of religion, but a lifetime of the disconnection I experienced with God and my community of worshipers gave rise to a painful and unspeakable conclusion: I doubt the existence of God.

"Blank, do you know what happens to children who are disobedient and non-believers?"

"No, Sister Stella."

"If you die in sin without repenting and accepting God's love you will go to purgatory or descend into the fires of hell and live with Satan for an eternity as we are warned in a passage from the Book of Revelation.

'But the fearful, and unbelieving, and the abominable, and murderers, and whoremongers, and sorcerers, and all liars, shall have their part in the lake which burneth with fire and brimstone' (Revelation 21:8).

Blank, we must all try to be obedient and remain faithful to God."

"Yes, Sister."

Although it's been many years since I was a first grader in Sister Stella's class her lessons remain deeply entrenched in my psyche and as a result of my religious education and personal life experience I've developed my own unorganized and peculiar belief system. My beliefs control my personal journey and affect my worldview. What I believe in is the power of energy and the impact that energy has on man. According to Einstein, "energy cannot be created or destroyed; it can only be changed from one form to another." Since energy is indestructible I believe that each of us live on for eternity in some unknown nature; and that everything in the universe, whether seen or unseen, exists as a result of this indestructible energy.

Studies demonstrate that the positive and negative emotions of each of us are contagious, constantly being absorbed or exchanged. Energy such as love and generosity flowing into universe contributes to harmony and, conversely, energy such as hatred and greed contributes to dissonance in the world. Moreover, collective consciousness or group intentions affect change on an observable level. A powerful force of energy is created when a unifying group shares a vision, prayer, hope or dream. I believe that if we could channel a collective consciousness of love and peace – we can change the world.

Studies also demonstrate that the negative energy of depression can infect the minds and spirits of others. I'm remorseful that my depressed emotions have emitted negative energy into the universe, however my remorse serves as a motivator to change whatever can be changed so that I'm not poisoning anyone like a toxic fume.

I also believe that powerful positive energy and visualization could promote healing. In 1996 my father remained unconscious and on life support for over one month as a result of unanticipated complications from open heart surgery. The weeks following his surgery progressed into the holiday season. The holiday season has always been an emotional time of year for me and on this mournful Christmas my emotional energy was all-encompassing and boundless. I hoped with all my heart for the special magical transformation that the season promises.

I directed some of that energy into positive visualization to promote my father's healing. I looked beyond all of the life sustaining equipment and focused on the area of my father's chest that was closest to his heart and lungs and began to look inside his body. I then visualized his ribcage moving up and down as he took each breathe; and envisioned his heart and lungs pumping healthy blood and energy throughout his body. I also prayed even though I have little faith. My agnostic mentality leaves me torn between belief in God and atheism and sometimes I resort to prayer just in case I'm being heard.

Many weeks later, my father began to recover and I believe his recovery was possible because of science, the powerful energy of collective intentions, positive visualization, prayer and love.

It took many more months of rehabilitation before my father was weaned off of the ventilator and his speech and motor skills were strengthened. In the interim, physical therapists helped him regain the use of his hands so that he could communicate through writing. I recall the day that the doctors informed me that he could finally begin to communicate brief messages through writing.

"Dad, we haven't been able to exchange words for a very long time and I can't wait to find out what you've been thinking."

I waited in anticipation for my father's words of wisdom as he struggled to scribble the following words on paper:

"What I think about every day is a nice cold beer."

As time progressed my father was able to expand upon his writing and I saved one of his notes, dated January 13, 1998, in my keepsake box which I will share with you.

"You did more these last few weeks than I thought you could ever do...you see me every day and bring me love, thank you...."

Over the next decade our lives became even more complicated and I don't know if my father felt the same way when he passed away from cancer on March 16, 2006. In a strange way I wish we parted on that cold January day so many years before because at least I would be sure that he knew that I loved him. I hope that the energy of the love that my father and I once shared exists somewhere in the universe and that I could find a way to connect to it one day.

At times I take my theory of energy a step further into absurdity by believing that inanimate objects possess varying degrees of good and evil power. Perhaps my religious studies opened my mind to magical thinking even though Catholics believe that superstitions are evil. Many people accept that inanimate objects carry human qualities in the figurative sense, but I believe it in the most literal sense. When good energy has inhabited an object, like a treasured gift or keepsake, I feel a sense of balance and light. However, when evil energy has inhabited a particular object, I feel a sense of unrest and darkness. Some may say that I'm superstitious, but I believe that my personification of inanimate objects is extreme and most likely borders on psychological dysfunction.

In the late 1980's I interviewed for a position as an Administrative Assistant to the President of one of the twenty most admired companies in the world located on one of the top floors of The World Trade Center in New York City.

"Blank, I see that you have several years of experience as an assistant to the senior partner of a prestigious law firm. We are looking for a candidate with your background. We can offer you a generous salary, training and mentoring programs, and an excellent employee benefit package."

"Your offer is impressive and beyond anything I ever anticipated, however, I must decline for personal reasons."

If I were able to be completely forthcoming I would have explained that I had an unanticipated irrational fear of being inside or even close to the massively tall building. While on the interview I could not shake the feeling that something extremely destructive would someday occur on their premises. I didn't know if I was feeling apprehensive because of a new phobia of heights or my long-held belief that some inanimate objects hold evil energy, although I never possessed a strong predisposition towards believing that energy existed in mortar and steel. Back then I certainly never conceived of the notion that the World Trade Center was a target for evil conspiracy.

As we all know, on September 11, 2001 nearly 3,000 innocent people lost their lives in the World Trade Center terrorist attacks and the long term physical and psychological effects are still incalculable well over a decade later. Through my terror and grief on that fateful morning, I was just beginning to understand terrorism and its cataclysmic evil energy.

My beliefs and thoughts on the subjects of suffering and evil contribute to the darkness of my depression. There is a need for religion in a world where violence has touched our country, schools and neighborhoods. The Church is a place of refuge for many who are in pain, however when the current news casts an even darker shadow on my depression I am unable to turn to the Church for solace - so I swallow the pain alone.

Recently Blank2 suggested that I go back to Church on a day I was feeling deep doubts about the existence of God.

"Blank, you are a spiritual person and going to Church may help your depression."

"I don't believe in God. Whenever I try to pray I feel nothing but emptiness"

"Maybe you're just feeling angry at God."

"I'm not angry at God because He does not exist. I'm feeling angry about my life and the emptiness of my existence. I will not go back to Church!"

"Blank, do you think that I'm speaking out of my ass? If you make a commitment to a more spiritual life you can fill some of the void. I only gave you an assignment on one other occasion when I asked you to write on the subject of hope and look how wonderful that turned out."

I was startled because Blank2 rarely becomes adamant about anything and the distraction of his cuss snapped me out of my deep introspection and awakened all my senses for a moment. It's amazing how a cuss can affect a person. If truth be told there is a part of me that aches to believe in God and I speculate that there is a part of him that doubts because neither of us can demonstrate with certainty that God does or does not exist. The primary cause of my depression is my feelings of deprivation of significant love and perhaps love can be found somewhere in a community of worshipers. I do know that Church rituals, like weddings and funerals, continue to hold deep spiritual meaning in my life. I think I owe it to Blank2 and myself to visit a place of worship once again. The ability to connect to Blank2 when I wrote on the subject of hope helped me to feel a little less lonely so perhaps I just need to have a little more faith in his assignment.

Whether we are religious or atheist I think most of us agree that the *reason for our existence* is to bring some good into the world even if we are only capable of contributing in small ways. The accumulation of small good deeds can change the world. I told Blank2 during our session on my belief system that I do believe in something magnificent and prevailing - I believe in the power of the goodness of people - and I believe that we could create heaven on earth.

Reflections on Chapter 2: Believe

All of us live out our days with threats of sickness, humiliation, abandonment, aging and death. As a person who lives with deep doubts about the existence of God, I especially feel the hopelessness of the human condition because I often believe that God will not keep me safe, that there is no promise of an afterlife and that He is not listening to my solemn prayer. I persevere through my own inner strength and the therapeutic alliance; however, when I am weak and my support has waned - I am overcome by an unearthly misery.

Theists ask why I choose to doubt since individuals without religious affiliation are at a higher risk for depression. My response is that my religious beliefs are not a choice in the same way that feelings of love or attraction are not a choice. Certainly there are things that I can do to try and strengthen my faith, like going back to the Church or exploring alternate religions, but even so I speculate that I am not capable of believing in God and, perhaps, I'm not even capable of forming a strong human relationship.

My religious viewpoints absolutely contribute to my depression but it is not the cause of it. Depression is a mental illness regardless of race or religion. As a depressive I unquestionably need to believe in something that will give my life meaning and purpose and lessen my emotional pain, but that does not validate the existence of God. So for now, when my world becomes dark and there is nothing left to hold onto - I try to believe in the power of possibilities.

Chapter Three

MUTE

The moment Sr. Mary stepped out of the role of educator and into the role of counselor something that was generated from deep within shifted and my voice was irretrievably silenced. Decades passed before I had a murky understanding of why I suddenly dove deep into the silent, still waters. How could anyone dredge up the complicated genetic and environmental underpinnings of their dysfunctional behavior given that strengths and weaknesses are carelessly passed down from generation to generation in subtle ways unknown to us?

"Blank, I hope you don't mind that I'm keeping you after class for a few minutes but I'm concerned about you. I noticed that you seldom talk to your classmates or even look up from your desk. Is there something wrong at home?"

I began to sink into my seat while a blissful feeling of being nurtured mixed with a strong dose of fear and humiliation was churning in my gut. Sr. Mary's approach was the antithesis of the school principal's legendary hardhearted, brutal manner and the noninterference of my teachers before her. It was the first time in my life that anyone had compassionately addressed my idiosyncrasies and the human connection was to me - unearthly. I was immediately drawn to Sr. Mary like a bee to sweet nectar.

No matter our age, there are times in our lives when an ordinary event inexplicably touches our hearts and gives rise to feelings, behaviors and insights never experienced before. I don't know precisely what in my short life contributed to my insights or my behavior, but somehow by the fifth grade I realized that a genuine emotional connection was a rare gift and I didn't want to say or do anything that would shatter the fragile moment. I yearned to cultivate a bond with Sr. Mary, but I didn't have the emotional maturity to make sense of the sudden onslaught of thoughts and feelings and articulate them properly. I started to become more and more anxious about being the center of attention and not having access to a definitive answer. And so it went that when I tried to vocalize a response to Sr. Mary's question my voice became trapped inside of my inner turmoil and stifling dead silence filled the air, like a song left unsung.

For the next couple of years I remained painfully silent in the classroom, regardless of whether I was sick, hurt or needed to use the restroom. The very moment Sr. Mary reached out to help me I became two Blanks: the Blank who was mute in the classroom and the Blank who was able to speak beyond the school grounds. The outside world saw me with two vastly different personalities while my inner reality was suffering in anguished confusion. I was a fifth grader with a crisis of identity which would become permanently stamped into my personality. I felt intensely guilty for deceiving everyone, but it was entirely out of my control.

Even my tears were quieted and lifeless. Underneath my temperamental behavior and growing sensitivities to noise and all kinds of external stimulation, I was unable to dredge up those deep emotions that bring the wetness to the eyes that cleanse the soul. My heightened sensitivities surpassed other emotions and as a result I became numb to my everyday life circumstances, like my mother's progressive illness and struggles at school.

I became an easy target for school bullies; defenseless against their taunts and jeers because I did not have a voice to defend myself. I had a streak of confidence at home but once I was in my classroom I shriveled down to a frightened young girl, becoming smaller and smaller with each passing day until I became invisible. I fantasized about what it would be like to effortlessly participate in school activities and laugh with my classmates. I wanted nothing more than to be normal and accepted, but instead I was trapped inside my own head with my obsessive fears and preoccupations while my academics dramatically suffered. Each day I sank into a dense fog, faintly aware of lessons being taught, sounds of chalk against the blackboard and the rumbling of students moving around in their oversized desks. In hindsight it's clear that it's almost impossible for a child to concentrate on academics when she is silently suffering from an undiagnosed and untreated disorder.

The seventh grade finally rescued me from the wasteland and returned me to the world of the living. What helped me to move forward, despite the low probability, was that I was able to rekindle a friendship with a classmate and find acceptance among boys. I can attest that one friend can make all the difference to a child who is an outcast. Eventually I began dating and I even encountered some of the desirable imprudent experiences of adolescence. However, I continued to suffer from anxiety disorders and low self-esteem, always fearing that I will be rejected all over again.

My abnormal behavior was never diagnosed back then, but today I recognize that I was suffering from a condition known as selective mutism, whereby a child is physically capable of speaking and has the desire to speak but is psychologically unable to speak under certain circumstances. Most children with selective mutism suffer from severe anxiety disorders, including fears of abandonment and social phobias. Many exhibit signs such as extreme anxiety, moodiness, sleep disorders and moments when their temperament becomes severely inhibited. Some children with selective mutism suffer from a sensory processing disorder and may be sensitive to sounds, smells and lights. The severe anxiety from processing all of the sensory stimuli can cause a child to become inhibited in unfamiliar situations.

Unfortunately my untreated selective mutism and sensitivities in childhood paved the way to my adult anxiety disorder and social phobia. Since I am highly sensitive to the emotions of others as well as everyday stimuli I become easily anxious and overwhelmed. Sometimes the feeling becomes physically jolting, as if electrical shocks are flowing deep within my muscles. As a result of these uncomfortable feelings I tend to avoid intimate relationships. I don't want to feel isolated and lonely. I am just trying to dodge being swallowed by the universe.

While protecting my limited emotional resources, I work on overcoming my social anxiety and sensitivities by finding manageable ways to socialize and also by spending significant time alone so I can regain my equilibrium. It's a constant effort to remain connected to people, but it is worth the struggle because paradoxically communication brings joy into my life and may actually be keeping me alive. At times I even find myself foolishly babbling with friends or colleagues because I'm afraid a silent moment may become irreversible. But there are still those moments, regardless of my best efforts, when my voice becomes lodged in my throat and I feel like an entrapped, muzzled animal all over again.

Reflections on Chapter 3: Mute

As I reflected on this chapter it occurred to me that the writing of my book has become a saving grace. Writing satisfies a fundamental need for freedom of expression without fear of being judged and criticized. When writing I find a connection to the mute Blank of years ago, reflective and obsessively examining thoughts and feelings. However, today I feel empowered by the reflective silence and I've learned to honor the mute Blank because she has helped me to understand human struggle and engage with the outside world more authentically.

Fortunately, there is help for children with selective mutism today. If a child is particularly vulnerable to extreme withdrawal at home or in the classroom, seek help from a specialist who is familiar with selective mutism so that the child could develop proper coping skills. If the disorder is untreated an entire life could become stifled, like a beautiful song that was left unsung.

Chapter Four

THE PLAYGROUND OF LIFE

The story of my big brother and me was written long before we were born, prior to descriptive words that come with increased knowledge. It's a universal story of how a mother's affliction with chronic illness sets the stage for family dynamics, sibling relationships and lifelong psychological repercussions.

My brother was eleven and I was seven when he invited me to play in our backyard. The expanse behind our house was charming and private, but it was inconvenient for recreational use. It rested about 40 feet below our living space making it a burdensome task to tote any of our wares down the steep concrete steps, so it remained, for the most part, a non-functional and uninhabited piece of real estate.

When we opened the heavy entrance gate of the red cedar privacy fence it scraped against the slate patio making a loud screeching sound. Dad told us that thick cedar wood was the best type of wood fence that money could buy because it was least likely to warp and break. The fence stood approximately eight feet high with a decorative lattice resting at the top making it difficult to see anything on the other side of the fence especially at my pint size.

As we stood by the front gate the backyard appeared almost bare, except for the ominous shadows that were cast on the ground, my brother's taller shadow stretched out beside mine. A modest garden with shrubs and thorny, tired pink roses stood against the backdrop of the dismal grey stucco foundation. The grass along the parameter of the yard bore wild yellowy-orange and ashen dandelions which I speculated nature created for the pleasure of little girls to unreservedly gather without reprimand. Oftentimes I created colorful bouquets or plucked the ashen variety so that I could blow all the seeds off the tuft in one breath with hopes that a wish may come true.

"Look Louis, if I wave my hand the shadow waves too and if I move my leg the shadow moves its leg."

"Blank, try and catch my shadow while I run around the yard."

On that steamy summer day my brother and I played with our shadows with a childhood sense of wonder, observing as the shadows became smaller and thicker and taller and thinner. Back then we didn't have video games or computers to keep us busy so we learned to occupy ourselves using our imagination. The days seemed so much longer then because every experience was novel and immersed in memorable richness.

The fact of the matter is that Louis is four years my senior so he wasn't going to be entertained by shadows for too long. As I was running around chasing my brother's shadow I heard an abrupt change in sound as his shadow disappeared. The thud of my brother's footsteps and the loud snap of the gate latch abruptly replaced the calm echoes of giggles and gentle strides. I began to feel queasy from the sudden change to my senses, one minute the world was full and blissful and the next I was a lone shadow standing in fear. I ran to the door to follow my brother when I realized that I was locked inside our gated fortress.

"Louis, I'm going to tell on you," I screamed.

"Blank, dad won't be home until late tonight and mom won't realize that you're missing until dinner time."

The predicament of being alone and trapped in an enclosed space terrified me. I frantically jiggled the gate locks, rammed the door with my knees and tried prying it open with all my might but my efforts were futile because dad's quality cedar fence was constructed to withstand hurricanes, earthquakes and conceivably a nuclear attack. There was no way out and I wouldn't be rescued anytime soon because during those long summer days my brother and I roamed the neighborhood unrestrictedly from dawn to dusk and as a result no one would immediately notice that I've gone astray.

Back then I was afraid to be alone, always in fear of danger even when there was no immediate threat. I was afraid of a Russian nuclear attack, a widespread fear in that generation; and I feared the elderly next door neighbor, Mrs. C, who despised children, the schizophrenic woman who roamed the neighborhood shouting obscenities, and the most notorious monster known as the boogey man.

My only mechanism for coping when bad things actually occurred was to simply dissociate the event as if it didn't happen at all, never realizing that my terror was festering and waiting to explode. One instance was when a neighborhood teenager was struck by a car on our corner while driving a moped and I completely detached myself from my emotions and fear; yet today I can still visualize with clarity the aftermath of the accident scene, the chalked outline of the resting position of the young boy's body when he took his final breath, the horrific blood stains which lingered for days, and the grieving families whose lives were forever changed.

But my deepest fear most likely wasn't about the external occurrences but a subconscious fear that existed within my very core. What I was really afraid of was being alone and trapped with my self-hatred. I was too incompetent to find pleasure in spending time alone to explore the world independently and to learn to become a friend to myself. The trauma that I experienced over being trapped in my backyard was a metaphor for my powerlessness to escape the demons that existed within. So when I became imprisoned in my own backyard I desperately needed to find a way to escape from the budding emotional prison that I was creating for myself and the physical prison that my brother created for me.

I scoured every panel and corner of the fence on that sweltering summer day while a swarm of yellow jackets and wasps danced across its parameter. If you ever waited for anything at all as a child you'll know that time seems to stand still. It seemed like eternity before I discovered a small space in a shady area where the property gently sloped. I cautiously wiggled my way through the slight opening and slowly and steadily began to see my neighbor's backyard and a passageway to freedom. As I eagerly lifted myself up from the ground I felt a sudden sharp burning pain on my stomach. I ran to the front of the house moaning while at a distance I could see my brother playing softball in the street with his friends.

34

"So you finally found a way out," my brother shouted with a grin. "Why do you look like you're in pain?"

"My stomach is sore but I don't want your help," I lamented."

"Blank, you have a large red welt on your stomach. You were stung by a bee. Don't worry it happens all the time around here. I'll help you."

I believe that my mother's illness left my brother and me without consistent nurturance and affected our ability to form a healthy relationship during early childhood. We were not close buddies which is understandable considering our four-year age difference and our radically dissimilar personalities. When we played together he was usually overly aggressive, although I always knew in my heart that he cared about me. At times my brother even took upon a parental role and provided nurturance, assisting me with bee stings, bruised knees and homework assignments. I, on the other hand, didn't understand then that my brother also needed nurturance and I neglected to fill that role.

From the outside our lives appeared almost normal but if anyone carefully observed our lives from the inside they would find signs of my mother's inability to fully care for the family. When I was old enough to take upon more responsibilities I either neglected my chores or overcompensated by attempting to incorporate a sterile and perfect environment which was perhaps a physical sign of my inability to salvage a sense of order in my life.

My brother and I continued to be independent from one another when he was a teenager and I entered adolescence. Like most teenagers my brother kept secrets but my curiosity about his personal life remained alive, patiently waiting for the privileged information to be revealed.

By the time I entered high school I realized that my world was also expanding. Transitioning away from the safety of my neighborhood and my elementary school was intimidating but I had hope that I would be able to work through my fears in my new all-girls high school located in the old established Rosebank community, approximately three miles from my home. The large campus included buildings that sat on hilltops and manicured property that stretched out as far as the Verrazano Bridge toll plaza. The private academy's freshmen class consisted of a small group of approximately eighty young women who lived in Staten Island as well as in neighboring boroughs. On my first day of classes I was overwhelmed with anxiety, wondering how I would adapt to my new environment.

Despite my trepidations my first days of high school were remarkably positive and the future appeared more promising than I could have ever imagined. It could have been a perfect time to evolve into a happy and confident individual, but several months later everything changed when I noticed several upper classmen mocking me as I was looking outside of the small glass window of my homeroom door. When I exited homeroom my high school experience unfolded into a life-altering nightmare.

"Whore!" a girl screamed as she pushed me against a wall. "You are a piece of worthless trash and we are going to make your life miserable."

"Why?"

"You don't deserve to look directly in my eyes. From now on whenever you pass me in the hallways you are to remain silent and look down."

"But I don't even know who you are."

"Do you hear that girls? The whore is still speaking. I think we should find another way to make things more clear."

I began to briskly walk away toward my locker but when I turned around to see if they were still following me the leader of the group came up from behind me, violently shoved me to the floor and repeatedly threatened me. The rest of the girls followed her lead as I lingered on the cold, hard ground while the girls were exerting their power over me. As the contemptuous behavior escalated I turned inward, withdrawing further and further, until all the demoralizing sounds and images turned into dust and my reality faded away. At some point I heard a piercing voice in the background.

"Young ladies, what's going on here?"

"It's her fault Sister C.," the girls said adamantly.

"Get up from the floor and follow me to my office!"

I followed the Dean of Students into her small office hoping that this incident would lead to my expulsion because I knew for certain that my life would become intolerable if I had to continue at the academy.

"Tell me what happened by the locker room."

"The girls provoked me, Sister, but I don't know why because I never met them before."

"Blank, girls don't instigate fights for no reason at all."

Sister C. listened to the rest of my story and then dismissed me without expulsion or advice on how to address the bullying - and I didn't believe that I deserved anything more at the time.

"Mom, dad, I want to transfer to another school."

"Blank, you always have a hard time around new people. Just give it time and I'm sure you'll find that it's not so bad. Why is your uniform torn?"

"Oh, it's nothing. I'm going to bed. If you can figure out a way to get me out of that school let me know."

I was beginning to keep my own secrets. I wanted my high school to be a new beginning but the upper classman almost immediately observed my weaknesses and exploited them. When I returned to school the bullying persisted and I was slipping further and further into a dark and despairing place. My bullies consistently antagonized me and as a result most of my classmates kept their distance fearing to be associated with me. I went through painful lengths to hide my predicament, making use of the less popular paths to my classes and avoiding the cafeteria where most of my classmates went in their free time. At times I believed that I deserved the social isolation because I recalled many times when I was ignorant to the hurts of others. I grew up in an uninformed era when bullying wasn't a popular discussion among adults so victims of bullying were expected to simply handle it on their own because it was seen as a normal childhood experience.

Somehow I possessed the inner strength to endure the bullying although it had an enormous effect on my studies and cemented my already low self esteem.   My issues of self worth were following me as I was beginning to find my own way in the world.

One day my history teacher, Mrs. R., witnessed the bullying and asked to speak with me privately after class. I assumed that she would reprimand me because I believed that I was partly responsible because I wasn't cool, pretty or smart enough.

"Blank, I've noticed that a group of sophomores have been hard on you. The girls come from powerful families which makes it difficult for anyone to help you. There isn't much I could do except to let you know that the bullying isn't your fault."

"Then why am I being targeted?"

"They're jealous of you."

"Why would they be jealous of me?"

"It's just something that happens when young women feel threatened for whatever reason. I think that you are an exceptional young lady and one day this will be behind you."

Mrs. R. understood the limits of the academic system. Even though Mrs. R. couldn't stop the bullying her intervention had a positive influence on my life. I was able to see things from a different perspective, a place of renewed confidence simply because someone cared about me. I wondered if the bullies had anyone that cared about them because if they did it wouldn't seem likely that they would behave so maliciously.

In time I found solace in a study area outside of the music room where I listened to Mrs. S. outpouring familiar pieces of music on the piano for the theater group. Each musical score was like the shedding of a tear and I felt cleansed. Mrs. S.'s appreciation for music reminded me of my father's passion for jazz and the big band era. At times he would turn the volume high on the stereo while belting out vocalized sounds of trumpets and saxophones; I speculate that this was the only time my father could release his heartache.

Oftentimes I found a group of amiable seniors sitting on the opposite side of the music room. I secretly enjoyed listening to their banter because they seemed funny, kind and cool and as time progressed I began to feel as if I personally knew them; and ironically one day I discovered that we did have a connection.

"A nice group of boys hang out at my house on weekends," I overheard a senior say. Billie S. is adorable and Louie C. has the most amazing sense of humor."

I was taken aback when I realized that the girls were referring to my brother and his buddy and excited because finally some of my brother's secrets were being revealed. Since my brother was older and always attended different schools it had been unprecedented that any of my peers would know him and what was more astounding was that until that moment I never realized that girls would be romantically attracted to him. I didn't reveal myself because I was afraid I would embarrass the girls and my brother; and, to be quite honest, I was being guided by my insatiable curiosity to discover more about my brother's social life. I became drawn towards my one-sided intimate connection with the seniors and felt a little safer around them simply because they were my brother's friends.

My brother eventually went away to a college in upstate New York. It was difficult for me to adjust to his absence because there was no longer a buffer between me and the sadness and frustration of our mother's chronic illness. Yet I serendipitously discovered that during this time our relationship did not weaken but became stronger. He was a long distance away from home and the separation gave us time to look at things differently and come to appreciate one another. He only came home during winter and summer breaks and I relished our late night games of backgammon.

In the course of time I attended a local University where I met new friends, discovering that the students in college were less judgmental than those in my high school. Like many young girls with low self esteem I began to search for validation through the attention of men. When I started my first semester I decided to end things with my high school sweetheart. It was a painful transition because I truly cared about him, but he could not fill the emptiness that consumed me. J. always had a way of providing simple solutions to complex problems and although it was an endearing quality I knew in my heart that I needed to move on in order to evolve.

"You look beautiful today," J. said, as he wrapped his arms around me and gently pulled me toward him.

"Thanks for taking me to the beach. I've wanted to come here for so long."

"Then why do you look so sad?"

"I just don't feel right enjoying the day while my mother is home alone and unable to help herself. Could you drive me home, please?"

"We just got here! I want to spend some time alone with you."

"We'll make plans soon. I really need to go. Let's pack up the car quickly so we can beat the rush hour."

"Blank, do you realize that if everyone drives a little faster we would never have traffic problems."

"That's brilliant," I laughed.

As I was expanding my life, I tried to find ways to fill the growing void. As the years progressed my relationship with my brother underwent further transformation and we grew apart as we were adapting to our new roles as adults. My brother became a successful Wall Street businessman, husband and father of two beautiful girls. Whereas, slowly and progressively, I permitted my youth and aspirations to pass me by until I was reduced to being just a fly on the wall.

In my late twenties I was hospitalized for the first time for treatment of my depression. The hospitalization was several months long and during that time I lost my job and then my apartment because I was unable to afford the rent. Thankfully my father allowed me to move back home but still I was becoming increasingly depressed from insurmountable losses and my inability to live independently.

I stood out as an enigma to family and friends; depression changed my behavior and my symptoms were grossly misunderstood. Every moment I was fighting a war with my own mind, dealing with an illness that tells you that you are weak and worthless. I began to navigate a complicated mental health system, even though I did not have the mental ability, and I was making devastating and unfixable mistakes.

It wasn't until I was in extreme crisis mode that I began to reach out to my brother, placing an even deeper strain on our relationship. One night I became trapped in a vortex of anxious and irrational thinking while I was home alone surrounded by my mother's treasured belongings, as well as the stacks of unpacked boxes and furnishings that briefly made their home in the apartment I surrendered in the wake of my hospitalization. The physical space had become a perpetual reminder of the heartbreaking absence of my mother and my loss of independence.

My sense of unease was heightened by the sounds of cars swooshing through the high traffic street of the Westerleigh neighborhood. A feeling of hopelessness came into my consciousness attached to my irrational noise sensitivity and I began to contemplate ending my life. I believed with every depth of my being that I could never find peace from my noise sensitivity and that my life would never improve. That's what depression does – it feeds the mind with negativity and provides all the proof that you need to support erroneous thinking. My thought processes were baffling indeed but the entire concept of suicide is mystifying because it is contrary to the strongest human instinct of self preservation. That is why, in most instances, taking one's life is absolutely the result of a serious mental disorder.

It was still early in the evening when I made a reckless decision to walk into the bathroom and take a straight edge blade from the medicine cabinet. I held the blade to my wrist for about twenty minutes while my mind was racing with hopeless thoughts and fears of the physical pain I was about to endure. Sweating, rapid breathing, heartbeat racing and trembling - I gripped the small blade and slit my wrist with a fierce and unshakable determination. When I looked at the damage I had done I began to reason that I definitely did not want to end my life – I just wanted to kill something unfathomably deep and dark. My slit wrist was a cry for help.

The writing of Sylvia Plath, American novelist and poet, resonates with me especially when she wrote about her attempted suicide by slit wrist: "But when it came right down to it, the skin of my wrist looked so white and defenseless that I couldn't do it. It was as if what I wanted to kill wasn't in that skin or the thin blue pulse that jumped under my thumb, but somewhere else, deeper, more secret, and a whole lot harder to get."

Eventually, I staggered toward the telephone and called my brother for help. I arrived at the hospital with my brother feeling humiliated because in a sense I had just jumped off a bridge and then sent an SOS while plummeting into the ocean.

My brother and I were not accustomed to confiding in one another so we kept our emotions hidden while we were waiting in the emergency room. I began to reflect on an experience that occurred when my brother and I were approximately ten and fourteen, respectively. We were in the living room checking out his old Lionel trains when we heard what we presumed was hysterical laughter from my mother's bedroom.

"Blank, I'm going to mom's room to see why she's laughing!"

"I'm following," I said excitedly.

When we arrived at the foot of the door we saw my father lifting my mother's head from the pillow while she gasped for air as she struggled to breathe.

"Louis, Blank, go back inside. Your mother is very sick and needs all my attention."

What affected me the most about that unpleasant incident was the change in my brother's demeanor, his lowered shoulders and sorrowful chestnut brown eyes. We then walked away and resumed playing with his trains as if the episode never happened. As I came back to the present time I believed that it was important to acknowledge our discomfort. I'm perpetually in conflict between reason and unreason.

"Louis, did I frighten you?"

"Blank, I've seen all of the Freddy Krueger horror films so this is nothing in comparison!"

The medical team that was treating me was unable to stifle their amusement at my brother's comment; and after they released their suppressed laughter it seemed that we all began to feel implausibly relaxed.

And so it was again that my brother attempted to help me in his own peculiar way however things were not as fixable as scraped knees and bee stings. I enjoyed my brother's sense of humor but I was scared and I speculate that he was too, yet we were still incapable of sharing our feelings. While I can't speak for my brother, I believe that humor is his way of telling himself and others that things arc really not so bad. When you think about it, as long as we are breathing, maybe life is more hopeful than we believe. Since that night in the emergency room I feel thankful that I'm the sibling with the depressive illness because I could not bear to see my brother with a disorder that would deplete his ability to see the humor and light in things big and small.

Over twenty years has passed since that incident and still my relationship with my brother is ambiguous. But what I do know to be true is that after many years of exploring the various playgrounds we have journeyed, we finally found our way back to one another in our middle years. After my father's death in 2006, my brother and I embarked on a new and closer relationship. Our sibling bond was preserved by a family history and my brother is now the longest-lasting and most significant relationship in my life. He continues to provide support through some of my difficult hurdles and I at long last attempt to find small ways to nurture his soul. As T.S. Elliot sagely wrote: "We shall not cease from exploration - and at the end of all our exploring - will be to arrive where we started - and know the place for the first time."

Reflections on Chapter 4: The Playground of Life

By looking at my brother's personality alongside of mine from childhood to adulthood I was able to begin the exploration of the environmental and genetic influences on my depression. Perhaps my brother developed better coping strategies because of our gender or age differences or maybe I was born with a depression gene that predisposed me to the illness. Whether my depression was caused by environment or biology is a complicated question but the most reasonable answer seems to be that mental characteristics are the result of both influences, and in my case, I inherited a vulnerability to depression. Regardless of the cause of depression, it is my hope that by understanding the attitudes and behaviors of my past I could adjust the way I handle difficult life situations today.

The writing of this chapter shed light on my lifelong relationship with my brother. Since my father's death in 2006, my relationship with my brother has become the most important relationship in my life, however fostering sibling closeness has been a thorny undertaking as we continually struggle to find a tolerable balance when my depressive symptoms worsen. Depression not only affects the quality of my life but it is a burden to anyone that cares for me. My advice to those who care for the mentally ill is to find support through education or advocacy groups so that you can learn to care for yourself without giving up on your loved one. Above all, remember to always find the person behind the illness.

Chapter Five

COUNTDOWN TO PEACE

The traditional melody of Auld Lang Syne awakens bittersweet memories of a time when I was enveloped by family and friends. The holiday was celebrated at my maternal grandparents' home where family values and Italian traditions were kept alive. Grandma Cristina and Papa Peter were the matriarch and patriarch of the family and they took pride in their sense of duty. My grandparents were strong individuals who earned admiration and respect among family and community because they bravely triumphed over the significant challenges of assimilating into the new country as well as empowering other Italian immigrants to bravely persevere.

Holidays and milestone celebrations were extraordinary moments in my youth when my colorful and vivacious extended family were together, creating memories that have become a lifeline to my past. New Year's Eve was a particularly memorable holiday in which my extended family celebrated life and love with great gusto. The focus was on an extraordinary feast where the elders enjoyed premium seating at the grand dining room table replete with vigorous conversations spoken in English and Italian; while my cousins and I sat at the adjoining children's table where the exuberance of youth thrived. The sights, sounds and smells represented an authentic Italian holiday as everyone indulged on lobster, mussels and clams served over linguine with a festive red seafood sauce. Papa Peter took pleasure in frying fish heads and manipulating a snail fork to extract the flesh from snail shells, or escargot as they are more commonly known in French cuisine. He also relished homemade wine and rolling Laredo cigarettes. I once wondered if Papa Peter was rolling marijuana because he always maintained an unusually heightened state of calm and well-being, remarkably evident because of the sheer contrast of his spirited family. In hindsight I realize that Papa Peter existed in this harmonious state because he was content in his love for Grandma Cristina and his large family. Papa Peter no longer maintained a peaceful state of mind once Grandma Cristina died.

I used hand gestures, facial expressions and an abundance of persistence to communicate with my Italian-speaking grandparents. Even though communicating through language barriers was difficult and infrequent I understood that I was loved simply because I was a part of them. I recall a heartwarming exchange with Grandma Cristina when I was approximately five years old:

"Mangia," Grandma said, as she pushed a bowl of linguini closer to me.

"I don't want to eat," I responded, as I shook my head obstinately.

"Pane e burro?" Grandma asked while holding a loaf of mouth-watering homemade Italian bread and butter.

"Yes," I nodded gratefully.

Grandma cut the bread with her bare hands and spread the butter using her skillful thumbs. It was a privilege to hold Grandma's attention and to be nurtured by her in this way. I speculate that sharing food is one of the most primitive and effective ways of connecting people to one another especially when there are language barriers. Grandma and I formed a bridge between the old and the young and I represented her legacy. Memories of holiday feasts help me to feel a sense of connection today, yet, back then, I often felt different from my extended family and somewhat lonely in their presence – perhaps this was the beginning of my depressive symptoms.

After the holiday feast my brother, cousins and I merrily paraded into Grandma's austere kitchen to prepare for the midnight revelry. Grandma Cristina doled out her old pots and pans so that we could celebrate the New Year with a bang. What struck me the most about the pots was that they bore decades of corrosion and remnants of deep fried Mediterranean cuisine. The patina was oddly beautiful because it represented memories that were burned into my grandparents' old cookware and depicted stories of epic proportions of the life and times of an Italian American family.

I was twelve years old when I celebrated my last New Year's Eve at my grandparents' home along with extended family and friends. Shortly before midnight we gathered in my grandparents' living room to watch the New Year's Eve party in Times Square broadcasted on their black and white television screen. The children plunked themselves down on the tattered carpeting while the adults positioned themselves behind us, the excess peering in from the adjoining dining room. The mysterious Madam X was dressed in black and stood quietly in the background. Madam X's identity was shrouded in secrecy which was never revealed to the inquisitive children. This particular year we watched Dick Clark's New Year's Rockin' Eve. The boisterous crowd was silenced as we viewed live footage of Dick Clark in Times Square counting down. Finally it was the moment we were waiting for and in unison we shouted the infamous countdown as we watched the New Year's Eve ball come down:

"Five – Four – Three – Two – One. Happy New Year!"

We hugged and kissed one another and then prepared to spread our joy with the outside world. On that wintery night nearly thirty people hurried out of the living room, through the narrow hallway, out the front door, down the brick stairs and unto a small concrete patio. We banged our pots and pans and wished neighbors and strangers a Happy New Year. Unlike the quiet streets of my community in Staten Island, my grandparents' densely populated Brooklyn neighborhood was like a city unto itself, bustling with life and energy. In those simpler times we were uninterested in celebrating with elaborate parties and expensive champagne; we only desired to bring in the New Year on a Brooklyn stoop with family and friends who were near and dear to us. On that night nothing could harm our family because we were invincible and inseparable.

The passage of time always brings change and sadly the abounding joy of extended family and friends dissipated. I assumed our family traditions would be never-ending but I realize now that it was essential for us to be purposeful in preserving our grandparents' legacy. The stark difference of then and now for me personally is deeply distressing. Today my parents are deceased and my extended family celebrate New Year's Eve with their immediate family and friends. I spend the holiday alone and it has become a time of self evaluation, reflections of my past and fear of an uncertain future. My anxieties are further exasperated by concerns for those who may be out on a night known for deadly car accidents. And, I fear the occurrence of a cataclysmic event like a terrorist attack in Times Square or where masses of people gather.

Years ago I was a patient in a psychiatric hospital on New Year's Eve experimenting with yet another round of medications for treatment of my depression and anxiety. I recall being alone in a darkened room as midnight approached wondering how I came to be in such a demoralizing position. It seemed that many of the patients were unaware of their environment because of their various psychological disorders, but I was acutely sensitive to my circumstances and I yearned to find my way back to that old Brooklyn stoop. That night I resolved never to be alone on a holiday again. Perplexingly, I was more hopeful about my future back then.

Each New Year becomes a little more discouraging as I realize that my circumstances remain the same. I no longer make resolutions given that I'm a middle aged woman who will never be able to have children or the large family that was always a part of my childhood dreams. In fact, all of my endeavors to live a more fulfilling life resulted in failure - and I have grown weary. Some may say that I'm a pessimist but I am attempting to be a realist so that I will not continue to be disappointed by the things that could never be and all that I am not.

These days my New Year's resolutions and aspirations have become more global in nature because despite all my personal losses I maintain a strong faith in humanity. This rationale exceeds the limits of my frail abilities because I am a part of something much greater than myself. My New Year's Eve countdown has transformed from a celebration of love and family to hopes and dreams for world peace. I feel guilt that I am a bystander to the greater good, but I believe that if I at least consciously work at attaining peaceful solutions in my everyday conflicts my humanity will evolve and the peace I offer will spread in unimaginable ways. Hope is a verb and it is my vow to take action and make a contribution. Sometimes change begins with one small step.

I recall the great promise of the 2011 holiday season when the final few thousand United States troops left Iraq. It occurred to me that although we were still far from being in a position to end all wars perhaps humanity was at least one step closer to peace on earth. While watching the broadcast of the New Year's Eve celebration at Times Square that year I was overcome when the commentators indicated that there were an estimated one million people in Times Square and over one billion people watching the live broadcast throughout the world. Cee Lo Green performed his rendition of the song "Imagine" shortly before midnight and John Lennon's vision for world peace became a brief reality because in that moment - the world was as one – as we collectively celebrated a global New Year's Eve tradition.

Although thoughts of peace on earth are reassuring I achingly yearned for my own peace of mind in my silent revelry, but warmhearted thoughts would not extinguish my icy chill. On this New Year's Eve and the many that came before and after, I hungered for human companionship. I remember the magnificent power of a compassionate touch, a sensation so responsive that it is felt even before the actual contact. During the countdown I cradled my dog in an attempt to expel the coldness of isolation, but I still felt the force of my blood pressure rising and my heart racing as the floodgates of my memories were released.

Despite these aching emotions I never want to erase painful memories because it is the only way to hold on to my past and the essence of who I am. Electroconvulsive therapy wantonly stole parts of my memories and did not discern the happy memories from the sad. For this reason I promise to retain all of the remaining remnants of memories that are burned in my heart, especially the days when the carafe was full and I did not crave the last sip of grandpa's homemade wine.

As Cee Lo Green was singing "Imagine" I stood up from the sofa because I could no longer contain the flow of emotions while the ghosts of my past and present were clamoring in my brain. As the clock was about to strike twelve, I gazed at the television and saw a reflection of a forlorn woman and dismally became aware that she was me. Finally I whispered the final countdown - to no one at all - as the orchestra performed the traditional melody of Auld Lang Syne.

Reflections on Chapter 5: Countdown to Peace

As I reflected on this chapter years after it was written I could clearly see the steady juxtaposition between hope and despair, darkness and light. I recall that when I reflected on the New Year's Eve celebrations of my past I was transported back to my grandparent's home in Brooklyn where I could almost hear the laughter of family, smell the sweetness of seafood sauce and glimpse at the patina on the aged pots and pans. These visceral memories evoked feelings of togetherness, but each time I came back to my current reality I felt a bone-chilling loneliness because I was so far removed from that time. The most discomforting thought was that so much of my family is deceased and it is utterly inconceivable to me that I will spend the rest of my life without them.

During the writing of this chapter I experienced a stream of mixed emotions like longing and comfort, isolation and belonging, sadness and joy, defeatism and hope, and finally disharmony and peace. It felt as if I had opened Pandora's Box and the outpouring of emotions would never stop. Studies show that releasing negative emotions can be healing but for depressives negative emotions seem to be infinite. Releasing negative emotions is necessary but depressives need to do so much more to achieve a healthier balance and move forward. I find it helpful to redirect my thought processes by forcing myself to visualize things that are peaceful, like the smile of a child, or by distracting myself with an activity, like reading or playing with my dog. This strategy only provides temporary relief but it is a step in a positive direction. Hope is a verb and it's our responsibility to take action for change.

Chapter Six

THE CHAIR

Fantastical, compelling and impractical are just some of the words that epitomize the voguish furnishings of my childhood home. My mother was fond of unique period pieces and acquired art and furnishings, albeit on a limited budget, that gave the home an appearance of grandeur. Particularly distinctive was my princess style bedroom and a vintage French provincial chair. I would have liked to declare my childhood home a museum after my parent's passing, but that was not possible. Today the artifacts only exist as part of my mental repository, except for the chair.

"Blank, my wife and I are not interested in taking any of these pieces. You live in a small apartment and don't have the space. Look into donating the furniture."

"Louis, the Salvation Army and a number of other agencies that I called said that they don't have enough room in their warehouse to accept all the furniture. Maybe we could try to sell it."

"I don't think you are emotionally strong enough to sell each piece individually. It would be like ripping off a Band-Aid in slow, painful tugs. Call a trucking company and we'll just have everything hauled away to the dump."

"Since it's an active street let's leave the sofa and some other items by the curb and see what happens overnight," I said hopefully.

"No one would want these old things," my brother said as he dragged the sofa to the curbside.

I needed to remove myself from the situation for a little while so I took a drive to a local coffee shop to pick-up coffees to go while my weary eyes swelled with tears. From the rearview mirror I could see, waiting by the curbside for the next garbage pick-up, the sofa, old vinyl records, used toys, tarnished souvenirs, school art projects, deflated basketballs and our shiny custom-made rocking horse with its worn out saddle.

When I returned within the hour I was baffled because the sofa was gone. Perhaps, I thought, my brother found a way to preserve a lifetime of cherished belongings.

"Blank, you'll never guess what just happened. Within minutes after leaving the sofa by the curb two men rang the doorbell and asked if they could take it. They said they collect vintage furniture and the sofa's uniqueness and quality was a rare find. I guess the furniture does have value to someone."

"Yes, it certainly does."

Today, a vintage white French provincial chair sits proudly in the center of my modest three room apartment. The design of this chair was known first in French royal palaces and then its distinct motif gained popularity in Europe and finally found its way to my family's home years before I was born. The chair's thick and plush cushion appears comfortable and inviting, though, its delicate form and intricate carvings impart a pretentious and unwelcoming air. For those bewildered about its function during my formative years, my mother made it adamantly clear that this chair should only be observed from afar. My childhood home was large, yet the presence of the chair overpowered the other voguish furnishings.

As I was growing up I resisted many temptations to perch upon this throne until one day, in a state of pure exhaustion and inattentiveness as a young adult, I was lured toward the luxurious white velvet cushion and surrendered to its elegance and comfort – an indulgence that seemed equivalent to eating the forbidden fruit. From this vantage point I observed my parent's home from a whole new perspective; and while I was in a trance-like state I noticed the front door was ajar and my dog was missing. I rose from the chair and ran out of the house frantically calling out my dog's name and within moments I saw that my beloved pet was hit by a car and suffered a dreadful death. From that day forward I began to believe that the chair had power and that it possessed vengeful qualities.

What I'm now trying to grapple with is why, since my parent's passing, I decided that the only furnishing I would keep was the chair. In my small quarters, the chair appears even more present and powerful than before. Despite my practical needs for additional space and a comfortable chair, I respectfully decline using it for its intended purpose; not just because of fear of the chair's vengeful qualities, but because I've learned that this chair also possesses benevolent qualities and its powerful presence offer gifts of insight and inspiration. A revered chair should only be observed from afar as my mother instructed years ago.

Perhaps concepts that I learned through religion and literature influenced my perception of inanimate objects; but most likely I believe that I need to give inanimate objects energy and life to fill a void. Today I recognize that my loneliness enables me to nurture feelings of familiarity and intimacy with my heirloom. The chair is a significant part of my past and connects me to a time when I had family and hopes and dreams; and it reminds me to find strength in this connectedness so that I can imagine and work towards a more hopeful future. Who of us can say for certain what is inanimate and who can say for certain that there is no hope for those in deep despair? If we can imagine, for a moment, that inanimate objects come alive in fairytales and movies - then why, pray tell, is it so difficult to imagine a more hopeful tomorrow?

Reflections on Chapter 6: The Chair

As I reflected back on this whimsical chapter I realized that I have been projecting thoughts and feelings of my relationship with my mother onto her favorite chair. Psychological projection is an unconscious phenomenon of processing unacceptable feelings by assigning them onto something else, usually another person but in my case onto an inanimate object. The chair's beauty represented my image of my mother before exhibiting symptoms of multiple sclerosis, a woman who was the epitome of glamour and impeccable style. Since I merely recall the image of a healthy mother through photographs and old stories I could only appreciate her beauty from a safe distance, just as the chair could only be appreciated from afar. Perhaps the vengeful qualities I bestowed on the chair are representative of the glamour and style lost by the grip of multiple sclerosis as well as my feelings of rejection and abandonment as I stood in the background of an unfathomable chronic illness.

Recent research demonstrates that children of parents with multiple sclerosis are at a higher risk of depression and separation anxiety than children of healthy parents. It is my hope that my story will bring about awareness of the need for therapeutic intervention in children of parents with multiple sclerosis and other debilitating illnesses.

Chapter Seven

MY CORNER

My bedroom was both a sanctuary and a place of angst from the age of three until I moved away from my childhood home in my late twenties. I once knew every crevice and hiding place of that room as well as I know the back of my hand. It was from this room that I embarked on my first days of elementary school, high school and college; nursed the wounds of my adolescence; and prepared for my first date.

My mother created a decorative space with sophisticated features mixed with a touch of eccentricity. The whimsical landscape did not reflect my personality except for the plastic birds that dangled from a thin wire on my lampshade, a gift from one of the McGuire girls, and a Jonathan Livingston Seagull poster with the famous motivational quote: "You always have the freedom to be yourself, your true self, here and now, and nothing can stand in your way!"

The most striking features of my bedroom were the views of the intricate stone patio backyard 40 feet below and the Verrazano-Narrows Bridge. The views were breathtaking but when, as a child, I stared out the window and allowed my eyes to drift at the stone patio below, I had an unspoken fear of plummeting 40 feet to my death. The frequent thoughts of plummeting to my death were most likely a metaphor for my feelings of loss of control.

Inside the far corner of my room was my treasured refuge, spilling with dolls and stuffed animals tossed on the hard wood floors. Oftentimes I carved out a space and placed my inanimate friends around me until I was safely hidden. As I sat with my knees tucked under my chin I could hear my trembling breath until slowly and steadily I became numb to the outside world. In my corner minutes tended to turn into hours and the universe stood still. In my corner I imagined a pristine world in which illness, hatred and school bullies did not exist. And, in my corner I imagined the person that I aspired to become one day. I was hopeful in those years.

A large wood canopy bed flanked by four high posts rested in the center of my chamber boasting the allusion of a classic princess room. The wall hangings included three dimensional comedy and tragedy clowns with bloodcurdling exaggerated expressions and a bronze plaque displaying the traditional children's prayer: "Now I lay me down to sleep, I pray the Lord my soul to keep; if I die before I wake, I pray the Lord my soul to take." I wasn't consoled by the idea that the Lord would take my soul if I should die in my sleep and I believe that my wall hangings were the cause of my lifelong sleeping disorder.

The most frightening element in my room was a full-length painting of a young girl wearing a vintage dress and Mary Jane style shoes. The young girl's eyes followed me around the room, the uncertainty of her facial expression contributed to her mysterious quality. She looked like the ghost of a little girl who exited from a grave and walked into an oil painting. Despite all my fears and trepidations it never occurred to me to ask permission to remove the painting from my bedroom until I experienced a pang of independence at seventeen and decided to make an adult decision on decor. My brother had just returned home from college and I asked that he remove the painting from my room the following day, even though I had an unspoken fear that there would be some type of retribution. That evening I awoke suddenly from a loud thud and the force of something that had abruptly fallen on top of me. The painting had become unhinged from the wall that was a few feet in front of my bed, flew through the posts and curtains of my canopy bed, and landed on top of me. Since the painting had never fallen before that night, I was certain that the young girl in the painting was seeking revenge.

"It was just a coincidence," my brother said.

"I don't think I can believe it's a coincidence. Just get rid of the painting right away," I pleaded.

I felt as if I had abandoned the young girl in the painting, a ghost I had known for most of my memorable life, but I could not keep her because her supernatural powers appeared to be evil. After that night I searched for strange stains on my wall, ghostly footprints and voices but I could not find the evidence that I was seeking. Some people may be cynical, but my experience with the painting expanded my reality. This phenomenon was not just experienced through my usual internal feelings, but with concrete evidence witnessed by my brother. When I am most connected to my spirituality, fully open to synchronicities, I feel an interconnection with the unseen world. In the case of my painting and those that I have loved and lost, I believe that their powerful energy lingers in an earthly realm and with the passage of time that energy begins to fade away and become an indiscernible part of the universe.

Perhaps some of the collectibles in my childhood bedroom became powerful to me because I felt so powerless back then. But, even still, my childhood bedroom offered feelings of family and an appreciation of the seen and unseen world. I wish I could go back there to reminisce about my formative years and confront some of the ghosts of my past. I don't know the fate of my painting, but speculate that it is on display in the home of an unsuspecting family; or maybe the young girl in the painting is waiting for me at the abandoned Staten Island dump site or the like. The most powerful ghosts of our past don't easily fade away, they just temporarily find another place to exist, then when we least expect it they find their way back to us and haunt our everyday lives.

Reflections on Chapter 7: My Corner

The writing of this chapter awakened an insatiable curiosity about each and every furnishing in my childhood bedroom, as if I would find answers to my lifelong issues tucked beneath an old floorboard. What I discovered was that many of my early thoughts, beliefs and behaviors have followed me across time: the fears, magical thinking, and the need to find safe places that beckon me to turn inward. Since these behaviors were maintained for many years they evolved into psychological problems that are difficult to remedy, however self awareness allows me to have some control over where my thoughts are taking me.

I was also reminded of the importance of my personal space both then and now. When decorating my space today I keep in mind details like art, color and sound, all of which have a profound effect on my mood because of my extreme sensitivities. One characteristic of depression is the inability to handle stressors; consequently, I continually strive to find ways to minimize the external stimulus which produce negative physical and mental responses. Studies show that tranquil environments can reduce stress hormones which affect anxiety and depression.

Chapter Eight

SNAPSHOTS

As I sifted through my paternal grandparents' curios several years ago I came across a pair of miniature men's saddle shoes about the size of my forefinger and cradled them in my hands while smiling affectionately. Years ago my brother made our beloved grandfather a birthday cake and the saddle shoes served as a cake topper. It is often the case that my memories of the trivial and mundane turn out to be significant tools in understanding the person I have become today. Since I've lost so much of my personal memories, I've learned to cherish those that survived even when I bring to remembrance painful moments of my past. My memories are now enshrined in my heart's treasure chest.

Among my treasured memories are moments in my life when I was nurtured, advocated and guided by my family. I tend to remember only the rare visual images with the most poignant emotional impact; sublime images that help us to understand that we are all connected to everything and everyone.

I see vague and colorless snapshots, for instance, of my Aunt Ruth guiding me while I read my first children's book as we sat on a bench in the backyard of her apartment building; and my Aunt Angie encouraging me to believe that I had value simply because I was her only niece as we stood by the gates of her church. These images rely mostly on powerful emotions and not visual detail because they are the snapshots of my soul.

Some of the earliest images I can recall are of my paternal grandparents' two family home in Brooklyn; my grandparents lived upstairs and my family and I occupied the lower level apartment. I was three years old when the moving trucks arrived to take us to our new home in Staten Island. I didn't want to leave my grandfather as he looked at me with tear-filled eyes and smiled. Perhaps my severance from my grandparents and then my separation from my parents and brother from time to time thereafter caused my lifetime issues with separation anxiety. Today a routine parting causes feelings of loneliness and loss because I often believe that significant people in my life will be harmed or will reject me and I will never see them again, even though intellectually I realize that our parting is only temporary.

Grandfather Philip was a proud and hard working Italian immigrant who arrived in the United States through the historical gateway of Ellis Island in the 1920's. He was a fine-looking gentleman with a strong physique, fair skinned complexion, large brown eyes and thick white hair carefully parted to the side. My grandfather, as well as many of my relatives that preceded my generation, bravely persevered through cultural and language barriers, however, I was particularly proud of Grandfather Philip because he was one of the few Italian immigrants who taught himself how to read and write in English, long before English as a second language classes were available. In his spare time he would sit on a stool by the radio in the kitchen smoking his pipe and listening to American baseball because he was convinced that he would learn to speak English through his passion for the sport. My grandfather's pipe smoking induced an air of tranquility in his small Brooklyn apartment as he took slow and steady puffs while savoring the taste and aroma of cherry tobacco. Eventually he did learn to speak English and even read the sports section of the New York Post.

"Grandpa, what are you writing?"

"I'm writing my grocery shopping list, but it's not easy for me to write the list in English."

"Why don't you write it in Italian?"

"Blank, how will I learn to speak to you unless I learn your language?"

"Let me see your list grandpa."

Everything was spelled perfectly except in the spirit of a true Italian immigrant he added a vowel after every English word. So grandpa's grocery list looked something like this: 'chickeni, cheesa, mcloni....'

I frequently visited my grandparent's home on a Saturday evening where we would gather in their informal living room engaging in conversations spoken in Italian and English. Sometimes I could understand the context of the conversation, but very often it seemed as if everyone was speaking gibberish. My paternal grandparents' home was always quiet and peaceful, a complete contrast to the clamorous and unrestrained atmosphere of my maternal grandparents' home.

My grandparents' dim living room contained intriguing vintage items like my grandmother's Singer sewing machine and an engraved wood radio cabinet that my father purchased with his first paycheck when he was a young man. At times we would sit on their cozy sofa and watch the wholesome entertainment of the Lawrence Welk Show. I always enjoyed grandpa's hearty laughter at American comedy sketches.

"Grandpa, I'm going to ask dad if we could go home now."

"Blank, I realize that you must have homework and you would like to see your friends, but I hope you'll learn to appreciate your time with the people closest to you or one day you'll live with regrets."

When I was sixteen Grandfather Philip had a massive stroke. My brother and I rushed to the Brooklyn hospital to see the man who helped rear us in early childhood. When we arrived at the hospital our grandfather lay almost lifeless.

"Grandpa, Louis and I are here. Please wake up."

"Blank, he's unconscious and hasn't been able to respond to anyone," my brother said despondently.

I continued to speak incessantly all the while hoping to get a response but the vile hand of sickness was slowly and steadily stealing my grandfather. Then, finally, I discovered a valuable snapshot in my grandfather's treasure chest of memories.

"Grandpa, do you remember when Louis made you a birthday ice cream cake decorated with a miniature pair of men's shoes?"

Grandpa's eyes began to open slightly and with great effort he murmured, "I'll never forget." Grandfather Philip passed away shortly after our visit.

I've often wondered if it would have been in my family's best interest if we remained in my grandfather's stable and loving home all those years ago. However, despite my mother's illness, my first generation Italian American parents were determined to live the American dream in a suburban community.

After we moved from my grandparent's home I formed attachments with numerous caregivers. Though I had a caring extended family there was never one figure that had a vested interest in my rearing and I often remained in the background of my extended family's household - craving to be home with a mother who was not ill.

Aunt Mariella, my mother's older sister, was a significant presence in my early childhood. I can still visualize the images of her laborious domestic work as she kept up with her visitors from early in the day until late in the evening. Aunt Mariella's home was the central place where my mother's extended family gathered for visits and it was also the home of my two older cousins who I adored. Aunt Mariella was a strict disciplinarian who was in the strange habit of presenting her demands in the third person. In a low and controlled voice she would state things like, "Aunt Mariella said, don't touch." Even the naughtiest of all my cousins heeded her commands.

Aunt Mariella often made herself available to me and my family in times of need. She came to my defense when my elementary school principal informed my family that I was unusually introverted; and she proudly attended my high school graduation when my parents could not be there.

Unfortunately, Aunt Mariella became distant during my adolescence as my mother's disease grew rampant because it was too difficult for her to witness her sister in a debilitated condition. When my mother became a resident in the nursing home years later Aunt Mariella gently confided that she would not be able to visit her there and consequently my hurt and angry feelings kept me at a distance from Aunt Mariella. Witnessing my mother's sadness over her sister's rejection reinforced my bitter feelings, but as the years progressed I observed that Aunt Mariella's strict demeanor waned into what appeared to be a passive guilt. In time I began to empathize with her and I was thankful for all that she gave me and my brother in terms of nurturance in my early years. Sadly, it wasn't until she passed away a number of years ago that I understood what was in my heart.

As I sat alone at her viewing in the funeral home I spoke to her as one would speak to their God in prayer: "I give thanks to you for teaching me not to run into busy streets after my ball, for giving me a safe place to stay when my mother was ill, and for being present when I achieved significant milestones. Please forgive me for keeping my distance from you through the years – I just didn't understand your perspective."

My ability to feel empathy toward Aunt Mariella helped me to gain greater insight into the whole of our relationship and it enabled me to remember our past in a different way, in a thankful way. The resentful feelings I had through the years clouded my early memories of Aunt Mariella and forgiveness, empathy and my willingness to look at things from a different perspective set them free.

Aunt Josie, my father's older sister, was another nurturing figure throughout my life. I see snapshots in my mind of her Long Island home, a place where I felt safe and loved. I recall our daily walks to a pond just a few hundred yards from her home during my early childhood. The pond was like a secluded hideaway with a magical feel; its water was deep and pure without a visible inlet or outlet. My favorite thing about the pond was seeing the ducks waddle to greet me with their flaming orange webbed feet and plumage as white and pure as the first snow of winter. The ducks had a friendly temperament and would follow me around the pond like a pet dog; sometimes they even followed me back to my Aunt Josie's home.

My Aunt Josie's husband owned a doll factory and dolls in every imaginable size, shape and hair color were bestowed upon me with regularity. I played, bathed and cuddled my dolls however I was frustrated because these dolls were not as life-like as my Thumbelina doll waiting for me at home. Despite my frustration, Aunt Josie provided a loving environment and I was blessed to share these moments with her.

Not long ago I came across a yellowed tattered letter written to my parents by my Aunt Josie when I was five years old which read:

Dear Sister-in-law and Brother,

I don't know if you will understand this.... I held Blank's hand to write you a letter and she was holding the pen with me. She is doing fine and is eating, thank God.

Mommy and Daddy,

I am having a very nice time....This morning I had my juice and cereal and I don't drink a bottle anymore.... I am eating all my food and I am getting big.... Love and kisses to Louis.

Aunt Josie resided in a Long Island nursing home for a few years before passing away in 2012. I called her regularly although I was not certain she remembered our conversations because she suffered with dementia in the end.

"Hi Aunt Josie, it's Blank."

"I don't know who you are but I know you're someone special to me. I feel terribly upset that I can't remember you."

"Don't worry Aunt Josie, I know who you are. I love you and will always appreciate all that you did for me when I was a little girl. Does it make you feel any better to know you are loved?"

"Oh, yes much better. I love you too Blank."

"I know Aunt Josie."

I also cherish the snapshots of those times when my brother was nurturing. One of my most poignant memories is when my elementary school principal presented an assignment to write a fundraising jingle. I was a terror stricken seventh grader, desperately trapped between anxiety and a desire to successfully meet my deadline.

"Why do you look so nervous Blank?"

"My principal asked the students to write a jingle to raise money for our church. They're using the award-winning slogan in our church bulletin. I don't have anything to submit and it's due tomorrow."

"I'll help you."

Our loud bursts of laughter could be heard in the distance as we brain stormed:

"Look at all our parishioners sufferin –
Don't you wish our church had funds for Bufferin?"

"Come on Louis. I would never hand in something so ridiculous!"

After hours of making up silly jingles, we finally formulated a jingle that I submitted to the principal much to my chagrin:

"We have your love
And we have your will
But we need your money
Or who'll pay the Church bill?"

Sr. Kathryn's countenance was perpetually red with rage, but the day I submitted the jingle she was pale blush with pride. In the end, however, the clergy decided it was not appropriate to use the slogan to raise funds for the church. But that's okay because in subtle ways Sr. Kathryn was one of my nurturers and the memory of her approval combined with the creative writing experience I shared with my brother are poignant snapshots preserved in my heart's treasure chest.

While writing this chapter, I found myself wondering about my own innate attributes as a nurturer. I am a woman without a child, but I still have an overpowering desire to nurture the younger generation so that they feel valued, heard and respected.

My two twenty-something year old nieces recently assured me that I was a positive influence to them when they were young children. My nieces are among the few living connections that I have to memories of my young adulthood and I enjoy sharing poignant family snapshots with them. Perhaps one day I'll tell them about my invasive treatments for depression, including the damaging effects of Electro Convulsive Therapy on my memory, however, I'm not certain that I will ever feel that it's the right time. For now I'll continue to find ways to express that they are loved and that I'll support them should they need me. I hope they will continue to keep special memories of our relationship in their heart so that they will always remember that they are loved.

Memories of my nurturers allow me to hear the birds sing in the coldness of my winter. When I reflect upon the snapshots of my childhood, I feel a visceral connection to all of the people in my past who loved me and who I loved.

Reflections on Chapter 8: Snapshots

As I read through the chapter, I was captivated by bittersweet memories of my grandfather and the significance of his final words: "I will never forget," in response to a question I asked about a handcrafted birthday cake that was given to him many years before. I wondered why my grandfather was only responsive to this isolated memory as he drifted in and out of consciousness on the brink of death; and I eventually came to the realization that the simple and long standing tradition of presenting a cake is treasured by everyone because it celebrates life. My grandfather's precious memory was of utmost importance to him because it validated that he was celebrated and loved.

It suddenly occurred to me that I selected the particular vignettes in this chapter because they celebrated my life journey. All of us long to feel that our lives have significance and our most treasured memories are of the times when our longings have been fulfilled. These are the spontaneous moments that are burned in our memories, both emotionally and visually. As a depressive it is extraordinarily helpful to me when someone affirms my worth because I am often unable to find it in myself. For those suffering from depression it is essential to find ways to combat negative thinking. Whenever I am able to reflect on some of the heartwarming snapshots of my life, my thoughts and feelings improve.

Chapter Nine

MR. UNAVAILABLE

I was spellbound by John's chivalry, refinement and fun nature when we first met at the university. John also respected some of my attributes and it was exhilarating to feel valued by him, until the storm moved in and much of his charm dissolved into the ethers. At times he became uncommunicative, jealous, prevented me from seeing my friends and distanced me from his friends. I ignored all of the warning signs of a damaged relationship, preferring to only concentrate on the good that was found. On a subconscious level I needed John to heal some of the hurts of my earlier years, but instead, over time, he contributed to them.

I had opportunities to date other promising men as a young adult but my pathological inclination to trust and be loyal to almost anyone who showed kindness to me prevented me from moving forward; and as a result I dated John from age nineteen until we were married at age twenty nine. I always felt strongly about the sincerity of commitment in my relationships so in the ten years we dated I never entertained the idea of dating other men although a few literally came knocking on my door.

On one occasion a college friend unexpectedly stopped by my house while I was working as a salesperson in the men's department at Macy's. I came home to find my brother casually sitting on the sofa watching television just moments before he dropped the bomb. The memory of this incident characterized my brother's seemingly indifferent and practical persona. He was always unruffled and impassive when all of my emotional walls came crashing down.

"I went for a few drinks with your college buddy, Donny," my brother nonchalantly said.

"How do you know Donny?" I asked in disbelief.

"Well, he showed up at our doorstep and told me that he's been asking you out on dates but you've been refusing. He looked disappointed so I decided to go out with him instead and we had a great time."

During those years I was still pondering my identity, overly sensitive about being judged by family and friends, and by no means wanted my two worlds to collide, especially without warning. This was a defining period of time when opportunities presented themselves in terms of education, career, friends and future partners. I didn't fully comprehend then that many of the decisions I was making would change the course of my life.

A few months later a similar encounter took place with someone who may have been a perfect partner but the timing was wrong. As the popular saying goes, "He was the one that got away."

"You just missed Steven," my Aunt Josie said playfully.

"Steven?" I questioned.

"He told me that he met you recently and you declined an offer to go on a date with him. He didn't have your telephone number but knew your address and thought he would stop by to see you. I invited him in for a cup of coffee."

I don't recall what was more shocking: the revelation that Steven was actively pursuing me or that my aunt trusted him enough to invite him into our home because she was ordinarily afraid of everything and everyone. My aunt came across some difficult times and as a result she lived with my family for several months until she found an apartment of her own. Each morning I would leave the house with warnings of how to avoid impending danger followed by supplies of antiseptic wipes in case I came in contact with germs. My father's only two sisters had fears of the world and I think I inherited some of their tendencies. My father and his brother, though, were credulous spirits who engaged with the world through their incredible sense of humor and seemed to fear nothing at all.

"Aunt Josie, you of all people let a stranger in the house?"

"I know it's not my nature, Blank, but he was an extremely handsome and respectful young man so I made an exception. You know his family owns an international business and he probably could offer you a nice life. He'll be calling you soon."

Truthfully, I felt an extraordinary connection to Steve. He began calling me routinely, but pursued me in a manner that seemed comfortable. The problem was that I had already invested years with John and I owed it to him to try and make things work. Perhaps the weightier truth was that the thought of dating a new man was terrifying. I asked Steve to stop calling me although I think about what could have been until this day.

I continued dating John with hopes that we would soon marry and have a family. From time to time John would tell me that I would make a perfect wife and mother of his children one day but he was just not ready for the responsibilities until after college. But even after his college graduation and the start of both of our careers were well behind us, we had no foreseeable plans for marriage.

So after nearly ten years of waiting for an offer of marriage, I finally realized that John was not seeking a deeper commitment. I didn't blame him, it's just something he didn't feel in his heart and I understood. I also understood that there was something inherently wrong with me since he continuously postponed marrying me. Any attempt that I made to discuss our future seemed to come across as an ultimatum. So I said goodbye and tried to move on. Even though I had trepidations about change and loss I somehow found the strength to try and create some type of new life for myself.

Actually, I never really was in love with John. I cared about him deeply but through the years I realized that he didn't possess important qualities that I find attractive in men, like emotional availability. In addition to being emotionally unavailable he was abusing drugs, a problem which was beyond the scope of what I could comprehend at the time. I'm ashamed to admit that I didn't fully realize that recreational drugs would become disruptive to our future.

Through the years I have asked myself why I stayed in an unhealthy relationship for so long and it's only with the benefit of hindsight and my reflections through writing that I've come up with several possibilities: Firstly, I needed to learn to love myself before anyone else could properly love me. Secondly, marrying John seemed to be an acceptable way to distance myself from the sadness in my family.   Finally, I was concerned that it would be too late to have children if I left the relationship and began anew.   By young adulthood my severe self esteem issues and unresolved fear of loss was cemented. It would have been best for both of us if he did not come back asking to make things work – but he did.

"Please, let's get back together and we'll talk about marriage because I don't want to lose you."

"But, John, this shouldn't come down to an ultimatum. I want you to marry me because you are looking forward to spending the rest of your life with me. And, if you really are ready, I don't want a long engagement because we waited long enough."

"I understand. Just wait, I have something special planned for us soon."

On June 20, 1989 we went to The Water Club in lower Manhattan. John disguised an engagement ring in a glass of sparkling champagne and proposed at the moment I noticed the ring.

"Blank, I want to marry you but I'm not ready to discuss a wedding date or our future plans."

And that was it.   John challenged the accepted standards of a marriage proposal by eliminating sentimentality. He did not utter any of the long awaited phrases like: I want to marry you because I love you, I want to sleep with you at night and wake up with you in the morning, I want to have children together or I want to grow old with you. Since I thought marriage would be a vehicle to a better life I ignored his loveless marriage proposal and his emotional unavailability. I assumed that his constraint of emotions was a sign of traditional masculinity but if I were capable of being honest with myself I knew deep down that John seldom had access to healthy emotions.

Most importantly, I ignored my own barriers to forming an intimate relationship. It appeared from the outside that I was emotionally available because I continually strived to provide nurturance and understanding but I'm beginning to realize that I was also hiding behind an emotional wall. The most obvious sign of my emotional unavailability was my difficulty with being physically intimate at times. The more ambiguous signs of my unavailability were my reluctance to explore my deepest feelings on my relationship with John, my mother's illness or my emerging symptoms of depression. It behooved me to explore these issues back then but the wires in my brain were crossed and I was in full blown denial. I desperately wanted to believe that everything I desired would come true so I agreed to marry John. In time, after exhaustive conversations, we set a date for September 1989.

While I was planning the wedding my family had been anxiously awaiting the completion of a custom-built wheelchair accessible home for my mother. Unfortunately three years earlier the contractor disappeared with my parent's life savings and the foundation that he laid stood barren until only weeks before my wedding. My father paid the contractor, however the contractor did not use the allocated funds to pay the crews for their labor before he disappeared. This left my father singularly responsible for dealing with angry laborers. The workmen ignored my father's attempts to negotiate a compromise and took revenge on my family. We were defenseless against their fiery threats and egregious course of actions. The crews organized massive illegal garbage dumpings at the construction site on numerous occasions in retaliation. We were legally responsible to immediately remove garbage dumped on the property, so my father hired private sanitation workers to continually clean the site. It was a hellish cycle.

In due course a private investigator located the contractor, but by then he had filed bankruptcy and was unable to return the money. In the end, my mother lived in the new house for only a few months because her disease progressed to a stage where she needed intensive supervision and we made the difficult decision to seek alternatives. The incident with the contractor took a toll on my father's health as well and he began to experience the first signs of heart disease. We had hopes that my mother would be able to enjoy a few quality years in the house that was built for her special needs, but time was not on her side.

It was heartbreaking for my parents to endure moving into a house that was built from hope and completed in despair. I wonder if the contractor felt remorse over stealing a family's hope. I wish I would have told my mother and father that I was proud of the courageous and dignified manner in which they endured their hardships, but I always had difficulty expressing my feelings to them, and, in some respects, I never appreciated their inner strength until after they were gone.

My memory is vague with respect to the next period of my life because I experience terrifying memory gaps spanning approximately twenty years. The invasive treatments that I was about to receive for my depression and anxiety caused devastating side effects. The treatment for severe depression is often worse than the disease. While I can't recall certain moments in my life, I can vividly remember the depth and breadth of my emotions during this time.

I had been promoted in my professional position and began to work demanding hours while my dad and I cared for my mother through the long and grueling nights. The difficult truth is that mostly my father cared for my physically paralyzed mother while I watched emotionally paralyzed in horror of the sights and sounds of a major illness. In the mornings, my dad and I exhaustedly took the long trek from Staten Island to Manhattan to work and though we were both despondent we never spoke a word of my mother's illness to anyone - not even each other. Our family was very good at keeping secrets. We just swayed hypnotically to the rhythm of life.

I didn't speak to John about the struggles with my mother because he lacked the maturity to offer support and I lacked the maturity to understand how essential it is for partners to communicate. Since I was thoroughly distracted during my brief wedding engagement I didn't dedicate enough time to carefully consider this phase in our relationship. In other words, I remained in a state of denial and refused to face the obvious truths about my relationship with John because it was too painful.

I was clueless about the notion that finding and maintaining balance contributes to a healthy lifestyle so as a result of working long hours, helping my parents move into their new home, sleepless nights, exploring nursing homes for my mother, managing wedding plans, John's wedding jitters, and preparing to move into our new marital dwelling – my life soon shattered into smithereens.

Reflections on Chapter 9: Mr. Unavailable

My heart was heavy as I reflected on my twenty something year old self being diverted by plans and dreams while unwittingly entering a mental battlefield. During that period of time I was juggling a busy life at superhuman speed so it appeared from the outside that I was thriving on chronic exertion. In actuality, I was suffering from an undiagnosed anxiety and depressive disorder, and when all of the external stressors became emotionally overwhelming I reached a breaking point. Almost overnight I went from being a successful young woman to an individual that was no longer able to function normally in day to day life.

Recognizing the signs of an approaching mental collapse is complicated because it varies from person to person, however it is far more crucial to detect early signs of depression long before a major breaking point. Depression still remains a highly unrecognized and untreated illness so if you notice worrisome behavioral issues in someone you care about seek professional help and become enlightened on the symptoms of depression so that you can help. Studies show that early intervention can increase the likelihood of a positive outcome.

I wish I could tell my twenty-something year old self to slow down and take more time to process some of the major transitions taking place - because her life matters. And more than anything else, I would like to offer her hope.

Chapter Ten

GOLDEN GATE BRIDGE

I never dreamed of a fairy tale wedding as a child, but instead fantasized about the love and family that matrimony engenders. I dreamed about adding an extended family to mine and I dwelled upon and achingly yearned for children – two boys and two girls so that they would never be lonely. Finally, after ten years of courting I was about to become John's wife and my dreams would soon become a reality. Although my motivation to marry John was not as uncomplicated and enchanting as my childhood dreams I was still ecstatic.

When many of our friends and relatives were informed of our upcoming nuptials their collective response was: "It's about time!" I planned my wedding in just a few short months and admittedly enjoyed partaking in some of the superficial preparations like choosing color schemes, venues and flowers; but these activities were a mere distraction to the elation I experienced when I romanticized my life with John after the wedding ceremony.

A dense fog with unprecedented thunderstorms enveloped the entire tri-state area on my wedding day, wrecking havoc on the ceremony and reception. The storm was a perfect metaphor or omen of things to come. My father and I shared a poignant moment as we waited for a respite from the torrential downpour in the limousine parked in front of the church shortly before the ceremony. My father never left my mother's side for too long, however, this day was an exception.

"You've been smiling since the moment you woke up this morning. I've never seen you this happy. You're glowing," my father said.

"This is the happiest day of my life."

I wanted to take this opportunity to thank my father for all of his sacrifices; for the times he attempted to fill the role of mother and father; for teaching me how to find humor and hope in pain; and for his effortless devotion to my mother. I wanted to say all these things to my father moments before he walked me down the aisle – but instead I remained silent.

Finally, we rushed from the limousine toward the church, but as I walked through the church doors I realized that my hair and white silk organza wedding gown were drenched. Normally I experience emotional turmoil when circumstances are less than perfect, but I was too blissful to be concerned about the small things on my wedding day. Instead of my usual pessimism I was able to see the world through rose-colored glasses and on this day the rain was a symbol of purity and renewal.

We decided upon a traditional Roman Catholic ceremony, except I didn't include bridesmaids and groomsmen because I felt that the short notice would be an imposition on friends and family. We did include a ring bearer and flower girl and my sister-in-law served as my matron of honor and John's buddy served as his best man. My father and I followed the small procession down the aisle and I was greeted by my fiancé who was clearly anxious as he meticulously used his handkerchief to wipe the beads of perspiration running down his forehead and unto his crisp white collar. Then my father symbolically gave me away.

Despite all the obstacles that the storm presented on my wedding day, the Sacrament of Marriage was truly a joyous occasion. Photographs were being taken and a video camera was rolling but I have not had the courage to view the video images even though more than two decades have passed. I observed every aspect of the afternoon ceremony as if I were a spectator watching from above and looking down. St. Teresa's Church was dark and dramatic; the pattering of rain on the stained glass windowpane echoed during the service; the air was filled with a peculiar sweet fragrance of freshly cut flowers combined with a pronounced mildew scent from the rain; I was honored to be in the presence of our guests who fashioned themselves in elegant apparel; my courageous mother looked lovely in pale pink chiffon - this would be the last time she would attend a special event; I treasured the spiritual music, the various bible readings, the exchange of vows and rings, and the nuptial blessing embracing a promise of love and peace:

...*Father, by your plan man and woman are united,*
and married life has been established
as the one blessing that was not forfeited by original sin
 or washed away in the flood.
Look with love upon this woman, your daughter,

now joined to her husband in marriage.

She asks your blessing.

Give her the grace of love and peace....Amen.

Perhaps my nuptial blessing was washed away in the flood that had accumulated outside the doors of the church on that stormy September afternoon because I did not experience the grace of love and peace after my wedding day.

My husband appeared to be less anxious after the wedding ceremony and I was elated about the prospect of our future. We reminisced about the heartfelt moments of the day and I was thrilled to let John know that my parents, brother and sister-in-law, Uncle Paul's family, and my godmother Phyllis gathered at my home prior to the church ceremony to toast our wedding day. We were even able to find a little humor in the fact that as a result of the inclement weather nearly all of our guests, including John and myself, were stuck in traffic and missed the majority of our reception. We were sad about those relatives that were deceased and could not celebrate with us – especially my cherished grandparents and my Uncle Joe who was the patriarch of my mother's family and taken away from us far too soon. I was most thrilled about the choice of band and singer who superbly performed traditional and popular music accompanied by the grumbling of thunder, my dad always had a penchant for fine music and I secretly concurred. We were concerned about our guest who fell and fractured her arm while dancing the Irish Jig. We laughed about how Uncle Charlie and Uncle Paul entertained the guests with their wild antics. We reminisced and laughed but sadly John never said

94

that he loved me on that day – nonetheless this was the happiest moment of our short-lived marriage.

John and I planned a honeymoon in Hawaii and San Francisco following the wedding reception. The moment I set foot on Hawaiian soil, after the fourteen hour flight, I was captivated by the scenic views of its diverse landscapes from the vibrant flora to its volcanoes and sapphire seas. It was my intention to settle into the hotel so that we could rest and enjoy the scenic places of this natural beauty the following morning but my husband had conflicting assumptions and immediately strayed from the itinerary that I had carefully planned. Our practice of communicating by assumption was already producing damages in our marriage.

"Blank, first I want to find a place where I can pick-up some Maui Wowie."

"What's Maui Wowie?"

"It's a powerful weed and its purest form is impossible to find unless you're in Hawaii."

"But we just arrived in one of the most beautiful islands in the world and we're on our honeymoon. Why do you need to get high?"

"Now, I didn't get married so you could tell me how to live my life. This is not open for discussion."

John's temperament changed in that instant. I wondered why marijuana was a drug that represented an image of love and peace back in the 1960's because I knew that his behavior was grossly inconsistent with that image and unquestionably contradictory to the love and peace the priest referred to during our nuptial blessing. My husband was extremely stoned on the first evening of our honeymoon and I was devastated. I knew that he used marijuana but I didn't understand the extent of it. In the last twenty four hours I had witnessed John's episodes of calm that quickly turned into fits of rage unlike anything I had known before. I suddenly realized that John needed to be on a constant high and that I didn't know who my husband was without the use of drugs.

I don't know precisely why I was beginning to understand the complexity of his drug use one day after we took vows before our friends, family and church. It may be because I didn't live with John prior to our marriage and never witnessed the entirety of his behavior, in fact we rarely spent more than brief hours together in any given day throughout our ten year courtship. John was educated, handsome, and impeccably groomed and he often explained his behavior away and all these qualities made it difficult for me to discern the severity of his problems. And, if I were to be completely honest, I most likely needed a marriage commitment before I felt safe enough to process all of the indicatory signs because if I had come to this awareness sooner I would have had too much to lose. Whatever the rationale, I was now panic stricken about my future and perplexed as to the exact reasons that motivated me to proceed with my marriage.

When we arrived at our hotel room I was hoping beyond hope that my husband would accept me in his heart and spirit and experience a natural high in our love and in the beauty of Hawaii. This would be the first time my husband and I would spend the night together even though we dated for many years. I'm not representing that we didn't have a physical relationship, but that we by no means spent a night alone together because my traditional parents would never approve. I was always a light sleeper and was uneasy about my ability to share a bed with my husband and I was even more apprehensive about my ability to satisfy my husband's physical needs. I experienced some problems in our physical relationship during our courtship and I hoped that the security of our marriage would reassure me and remedy my challenges.

As we settled into bed my racing thoughts and fears caused my anxiety to escalate. Eventually, he turned to me and attempted to have sex but my body could not accept him. It was as if I became a brick wall. The pain during his attempted penetration was so severe that I placed a pillow over my head so that he wouldn't notice the expression of agony on my face. I was mortified and couldn't understand what was wrong with me. I wanted to consummate our marriage with every depth of my being but I was physically and mentally impaired. I always dreamed that the process of forming a physical union with another human being would transform my loneliness - but instead it contributed to it.

John stormed out of the room. I sat back and waited for him to return, each minute felt like an hour. When I could no longer carry the weight of my shame and concern I got dressed and began to look for him. Heavyhearted, I explored the unfamiliar grounds of the luxury resort, sweeping through all of the lush amenities that I envisioned I would appreciate with fresh eyes with my husband as I was making plans for our honeymoon. Eventually, I stumbled upon a lounge in the resort and was overcome by the blurry scene that unfolded before me. John was sitting at a small table with an attractive woman intimately sipping cocktails. When he noticed me I panicked and swiftly walked away - but he did not follow.

Later that night, when John returned to our hotel room, I broke the angry silence by saying: "What happened tonight is a violation of our wedding vows. We need to be compassionate and supportive of one another and we need to communicate but you are unwilling to try and I can't fix our problems alone. This is a trip of a lifetime for me so I'm going to make the best of it and I hope you will too. However, when we return home I want a – well, I want a – divorce, unless you promise to get help with your drug problems."

After many years of a strict Catholic school education, I could hardly say the word 'divorce.' The Church views marriage as a sacrament that is indissoluble until a spouse dies. In Christian marriage it is sinful to divorce and in my traditional Italian-American family it would be considered a disgrace. My fury was the driving force of those courageous words. In that moment I felt as if my life was about to expand or contract.

"Blank, you misunderstood what you saw. Anyway, everything that happened tonight is your fault because you are incapable of making me feel like a man. No man could ever love you as I do because there is something wrong with you."

Suddenly, like a bolt of lightning, I had an epiphany. What John said was true and I was beginning to understand that I did not marry John because I loved him. I married him because I believed that he was the only man that could love me, even though it was a carnal love, and, perhaps more importantly, John was a vehicle for my escape from home. John provided a legitimate reason, a reason I could live with, to flee from some of the burdens and despair of being the daughter of a woman who suffered from multiple sclerosis. I had gone from the proverbial frying pan into the fire. What kind of a person was I to have such inappropriate reasons for entering into a sacred union?

After that difficult evening John and I tried to make the best of our honeymoon. I accepted his drug use and he accepted my inadequacies and from the outside we appeared to be the perfect newlywed couple. My parents had the ability to experience simple joys in the midst of their sorrow and on my honeymoon I was determined to do the same. I didn't know what tomorrow would bring, but I knew for certain that at that moment I was in one of the most pristine parts of the world and I decided to appreciate it with a full awareness. I kept a journal and photographs so I would never forget the greatest sensory pleasure of my lifetime and today the journal serves as a reminder of my inner strength and the importance of appreciating the moment even when life is bittersweet.

September 5th – Arrived in Honolulu in the evening

September 6th – Enjoyed the beach and surfers by the Kahala Hilton Hotel

September 7th – Went to a large flea market and absorbed the flavor of the island

September 8th – Visited the Honolulu Zoo, Pearl Harbor and climbed Diamond Head

September 9th – Arrived in Maui, went to a luau, visited Lahaina Historic District

September 10th – Cruise

September 11th – Para sailing, dinner at Swan Court followed by drinks at Spats with other honeymooners

September 12th – Private tour by native of Hawaii including the snow-capped mountaintop of Haleakala National Park

September 13th – Enjoyed pool and beach at Hyatt Regency Hotel

September 14th – Arrived in San Francisco. Took a ride on a trolley followed by dinner in Chinatown

September 15th – Fisherman's Wharf

September 16th – Walked across Golden Gate Bridge

September 17th – Flight back home

We spent the last couple of days of our honeymoon in California and visited the jewel of San Francisco the day before our departure. When we arrived at the landmark we posed for a photograph by an impressive monument with a sign above it that spelled out Golden Gate Bridge. Beyond the sign stood the golden architectural gem with breathtaking views of the city and towering hills. As we walked across the bridge I indulged in the beauty that was awesome to behold and reasoned that this was a place where dreams come true and wondered if there was hope for me and John. I had the ability to compartmentalize my emotions and until this moment I was not fully concentrating on the inevitable problems we would face once we began our lives in our own element.

Despite my grief I still longed to find a way for us to comfort one another. Since John's love for me was a carnal love I could never depend on him for emotional support. John's love for me was opposite from the kind of selfless love that my father showed toward my mother, a love that remained deeply entrenched in my father's heart despite my mother's physical decline. I will shamefully say, though, that John's carnal love for me gave me pleasure at times – at least he could love me in some way.

I knew that I cared deeply for John and I began to wonder if we could find a way to make our marriage work. If only he could satisfy my basic emotional needs, perhaps I could satisfy our physical needs and things would be okay. I did not expect a quick resolution, but at least a willingness to work toward a solution. How could we bring children into the world under these circumstances? I would have taken away years of my life if only my husband would have acknowledged that he cared enough about our marriage to begin a process to recover from his addictions. I would have supported him through almost anything but first he needed to want to change.

"John, do you think that when we go home tomorrow you will consider getting help or weaning from the marijuana?"

"I don't have a problem Blank. I'm able to work and I have good friends. You need to accept me the way that I am."

John was right. It wasn't fair of me to ask him to change his habits. I never respected women who tried to change their husbands once they were married and that was precisely what I was doing. I either had to accept my husband's lifestyle or leave the marriage. It was a hopeless situation and I was brokenhearted.

I walked toward a low railing on the bridge while the sounds of cars and pedestrians slowly faded away. I was slipping further and further away from reality as I gazed at the currents just a couple of hundred feet below. The bay seemed to swell with emotion whose sacred whispers vowed to fulfill promises of love and peace. Incapable of making a strong conviction of life or death I found myself passively surrendering to the flow of the sea. It was merely a sharp noise in the distance that deterred me from further thoughts of suicide.

Reflections on Chapter 10: Golden Gate Bridge

Over twenty years have passed since that day at the Golden Gate Bridge and although I did not commit suicide I endured a spiritual death that lasted nearly a lifetime. John and I divorced only months after our wedding and I never remarried or fulfilled the desired role of motherhood. When life was hanging in the balance I could have chosen fortitude but instead I accepted defeat. The tragedy was not the dissolution of a new marriage, it was the lack of resiliency, the willingness to let go of life so easily. Over time depression destroys reasoning skills including the ability to be resilient in the face of adversity. For many years I was angry at myself for my weaknesses but writing my book has helped to quell some of my self-critical thoughts as I gained insight on the symptoms of depression.

It is clear to me today that the period of time surrounding the Golden Gate Bridge divided my identity into two separate parts: the aspirant person that I was before my marriage and the disheartened person that I subsequently became. I wish I could go back to that watershed moment and change things but instead I am left to ponder all of the heartbreaking what-ifs. There are still moments when the pain is so profound that I am unable to avoid contemplating suicide. I envision returning to San Francisco and visiting the Golden Gate Bridge on a beautiful autumn day when the water is glistening like a sea of brilliant diamond wedding rings - fulfilling - promises of love and peace. The bay will greet me like an old friend and I will at long last reunite with the broken heart that I abandoned there years before.

Although the preceding paragraph is somewhat poetic I realize that it is the voice of my depressive illness. It is crucial for me to reiterate: depression affects reasoning skills and suicidal ideation is frequently the result of irrational thinking. Fortunately there is a pause in time between my suicidal thoughts and the execution of the act because I do not want to die – I just want to find peace. Despite all of my despondency, at this particular point in time, I feel that I can finally see the truth about the things that are important in life, like making a positive difference in the lives of others before my death.

It is difficult to recognize when someone is suicidal because it varies from person to person but often there are warning signs including, but not limited to, persistent feelings of hopelessness. If you believe that someone you know is at risk for suicide, learn how to offer support and seek professional help. Please do not blame the person who is exhibiting suicidal behavior for it is a symptom of a disease. And, above all else, remind the sufferer through words and actions that they are valued.

Perhaps the suicides of beloved public figures, like Robin Williams, will shed some light on the need for further research to better diagnose, treat and one day cure chronic depression. As a depressive each episode of a person's suicide becomes personal because I feel a deep connection to the victim. I understand the agony that brings us to our knees begging for mercy and the unearthly hopelessness we feel when there is no answer to our prayers. The suicide of another is an intimate reminder of the viability of this final option but I tell myself that these are the frightening thoughts of a psychologically unhealthy brain and in time the suicidal feelings will pass. It is my vehement hope that we find better ways to help those who struggle with mental illness through research, programs and our everyday interactions with those who are suffering.

Part Two

SLIPPING AWAY
FROM NORMAL

Chapter Eleven

INPATIENT

And so it went that a dark shadow was cast over my spirit and I lost my way. I unwittingly stepped out of a place of normalcy and into the dark and timeless abyss of madness. I did not have the ability to successfully navigate the chaotic and uncharted psychological terrain and descended deeper and deeper into hell at the age of twenty nine.

"Your husband's violent threat was cold and calculated so don't waste time making excuses for him. Take his words seriously and leave your home and marriage without delay."

These were the memorable words of Dr. S., my first psychiatrist. Dr. S. was a diminutive gentleman with a small and dark Manhattan suite which appeared to compliment his distinctive character. I started seeing him shortly after I returned from my honeymoon hoping that he could offer help with my anxiety and render advice on improving my relationship with John but ultimately he helped me to decide when it was time to say goodbye.

I heeded Dr. S.'s advice and also listened to the logical voice in my head that said I should leave my loveless marriage. I assumed John's threat was not serious but there was a possibility that I might be mistaken. I wonder if my life would have been for better or for worse if I had listened to the tender voice in my heart instead. I immediately surrendered my new marital home along with my dreams of love and family, but kept a wounded heart.

Even though I was emotionally depleted I needed to find the strength to consider my new living arrangements. My father would allow me to return home with open arms, but I needed a little distance from my parents so that I could learn to be fully independent and begin the process of building self-confidence. My mother was weeks away from being admitted into a nursing home so there were critical changes taking place in my parent's household. My relationship with my parents always created an internal conflict because I wanted to be physically and emotionally close to them but in the same breath I wanted to run for the hills. Suffice it to say that when I finally became independent from my parents upon my marriage, I didn't want to surrender my new-found liberation upon my abrupt marital separation.

I fought through the intense emotional pull of resistance and secured a new apartment. I was trying to move away from some of my old problems and move toward a better life, however in hindsight I realize that without proper guidance it was nearly impossible because I didn't have a clue as to who I was or what my role was in the universe apart from my parents and my husband. I was suffering from an identity crisis, the origins of which began long before my separation from John. I was disoriented when making decisions about my new life because not having a strong sense of identity was like being lost in the wilderness without the survival skills to find my way back home. It's very possible to find yourself when your spirit has lost its way at some point in your life, but what happens when your entire life has been off-course?

In the weeks that preceded my mother's transfer into a nursing home, I was overburdened as I dealt with family issues, my divorce, working long hours and establishing myself in my new apartment. I thought that if I just kept moving forward everything would eventually fall into place and my emotional pain would subside. I didn't believe that I had the luxury of taking the time to slow down because there was so much that needed to be accomplished and not enough time in the day. So I just kept going and going like the unstoppable pink Energizer Bunny continuously beating its burdensome drum, however my prolonged stress drained all of my energy until I was almost immobilized. I was about to find out that I had nothing left to give although this knowledge was not yet at a conscious level.

From the outside everything appeared to be going exceptionally well - however this is when the unthinkable occurred. Sometimes the unthinkable happens in a split second and sometimes there are long-term underlying issues that can go in an unimaginable direction. My long-term hypersensitivity to noise took me to the end of my tether. Since my childhood, random sounds trigger an exaggerated internal response that feels akin to widespread physical pain. Just the other day, for example, a glass bowl broke on my tile kitchen floor and even though I was not injured the sudden crashing sound slashed through me as if I were cut in a thousand little places by the broken shards of glass.

I recently did some internet research on noise sensitivity and discovered that I most likely suffer from misophonia, a noise sensitivity disorder where a person has an extreme reaction to certain noises. One of the causes of the condition is a sensory processing disorder where the sufferer's brain misinterprets information taken in by their senses. The disorder can cause a misinterpretation of balance, smell, visual cues and sense of time. One of the psychological reasons for the disorder is that the sufferer may perceive certain sounds as being out of their control which causes extreme feelings of anxiety and powerlessness. I experience all of the above-mentioned indicators. My noise sensitivity has affected my ability to function at work and in intimate relationships because no one could possibly understand how subtle noises produce physical and emotional pain. I would even go as far as to say that when I first shared a bed with John my fear of being able to tolerate typical noises from snoring or tossing around in the bed was as much of a struggle as my fear of sexual intimacy.

Unfortunately, I realized after I moved into my new apartment that there was noise from street traffic. I was preparing to go to bed one rainy evening but was unable to fall asleep because the swooshing sounds of the cars on the road exasperated my anxiety and contributed to an unmanageable distressed mental state. I walked over to the dimly lit kitchen sink and began to excessively wash my hands with soapy water as my anxiety grew stronger and stronger. My eyes were fixed on the straight edge blade on the edge of the sink which I had been using earlier to remove excess paint chips that the painters left behind. Then in a dreamlike slow motion state I picked up the blade and almost instinctively cut my left hand. Shortly after that I went to bed as if nothing had happened and got my first restful sleep in weeks.

I woke up the following morning at around 5:00 a.m., took a shower, tidied up my apartment and had a cup of coffee. I left my apartment in a peaceful frame of mind, never processing what I had done to my hand during my morning routines and throughout the long express bus ride to Manhattan. I typically recall painful and humiliating events over and over again, but I guess I was unable to cope with what I had done so I dismissed it from my consciousness. I had a 7:00 a.m. appointment with Dr. S. before going to my office and began the session by discussing my week.

"Dr. S., I like my new apartment and appreciate living alone except my anxiety has been severe. I'm constantly worried about my parent's well-being and I feel guilty when I'm not with them. I can't stop thinking about all of the recent changes in my life and I'm having a difficult time falling asleep at night. I'm wondering if I should take the Xanax you prescribed on a more regular basis."

"How did you sleep last night?"

"I had difficulty falling asleep and, well...."

Slowly the memory that I had dissociated from my awareness became known to me and I reluctantly tried to explain the shameful incident to Dr. S.

"Blank, up until last night you seemed to be functioning well under the circumstances. This incident is so unexpected. You need to go to a psychiatric hospital immediately to be evaluated."

It appeared to everyone that my fleeting marriage caused a sudden "nervous breakdown," an overly broad and inexpert label commonly used to refer to someone who is temporarily unable to function as a result of a severe depressive or anxiety disorder.

However, a relatively successful twenty nine year old woman does not suddenly and irreversibly cease normal functioning because of one difficult experience. If truth be told, it was the long-term struggles including the years of trying to make it through the agonizingly rough nights as we dealt with the later stages of my mother's illness. It is the prolonged existence of adversity that stealthily weathers the soul - the end of my meteoric marriage was just the straw that broke the camel's back.

My psychiatric hospitalizations began in a small New York City hospital that provided short-term care for people suffering from addictions, depression and anxiety. When I entered the psychiatric unit I was frightened but I tried to have faith in an intensive treatment plan. On my first day in the hospital I wondered if there were outdoor courtyards with beautiful gardens where I could take the time to reassess my life in a supportive environment, like the treatment centers I read about in books or seen images of in movies. Unfortunately it was not the therapeutic environment that I had envisioned but the small unit turned out to be tolerable. I didn't realize then that I needed more than a tolerable environment and antidepressants, I needed an effective treatment plan that included healing my mind, body and spirit at the onset of my first major depressive episode. Research demonstrates that there is a significant probability of additional depressive episodes when a patient has only made a partial recovery after their first depressive episode.

I didn't see my family during those weeks because my father needed to be at home caring for my mother, but two of my co-workers, C. W. and D. S., reached out to me and their kindness will never be forgotten. They had been at my wedding just a few months earlier celebrating my new life, love and partnership and now they were supporting me through the humiliation of my loss and my depressive illness. My co-workers knew very little about me until my hospitalization because I was always a private person. It's a distressing experience to go from being private to having your most personal issues revealed. C. W. still reminisces about the afternoon I returned to my office after purchasing intimate apparel. While I bashfully showed C. W. the contents in my shopping bag I heard my boss approaching and in my panic I threw the items out of my thirty fourth floor New York City office window. C. W. ran to the window and watched in disbelief as my intimate apparel floated thirty four stories down unto Wall Street.

"Blank, I can't believe that you threw your stuff out the window."

"Mr. R. is on his way in and I just couldn't bear it if he saw my most personal things."

Mr. R. was the senior partner of a prestigious law firm and he had more faith in me than I ever had in myself. It was a great honor when he promoted me from receptionist to his secretary, a position that required more experience and skill than I initially possessed. I saved a letter in my keepsake box that Mr. R. sent to me during my hospitalization in which he so kindly wrote:

"...Blank, I still believe that you are bright, talented, attractive and a nice and good person. The key to your future is that YOU must believe it also. You have great potentials – but you must 'turn the key' to realize them."

Mr. R. never saw my intimate apparel on that day but he soon witnessed some of the most personal and profound moments of my life. When Mr. R. was told about my marital problems, he recommended a renowned divorce attorney in New York City to accelerate the legal proceedings. It was an amicable divorce because I agreed that my husband would keep my heirloom engagement ring and our new home and I would receive a modest monetary settlement. I no longer wanted to protest my husband's demands; this was my peace offering in return for a quick resolution. Within weeks my co-workers C. W. and D. S. visited me at the hospital bearing a huggable stuffed puppy and my divorce papers.

"Just sign here and I'll notarize your signatures and your marriage will be officially annulled by New York State."

"Wow, that seems so quick. You mean all it takes is a few unceremonious signatures and my marriage is null and void, as if it had never happened?"

"Yes, an annulment is a formal invalidation of your marriage."

I hesitantly signed my annulment papers while feeling as if my marriage, annulment and hospitalization were just a flight of my imagination. It was even hard to fathom that a system would allow an individual to sign annulment papers while a patient in a psychiatric hospital, yet the reality is that it all happened and my marriage was annulled on that day. Legally my signature absolved my marriage but it's too bad that I couldn't sign away the painful memories as well. D. S. and C. W. left my hospital room and I held on to my stuffed puppy with the intensity of a child alone and frightened after a terrible nightmare.

In the days that followed Dr. D1, the Director of Psychiatry of the hospital, informed me that I was going to be transferred to a hospital in Staten Island because I had exceeded the time permitted in the short term care facility and he believed that I needed further treatment. I vaguely remember being transported by ambulance and driving through the front entrance of a large psychiatric center in Staten Island. Growing up I avoided going anywhere near this massive facility because of my fears of the unknown world of mental illness and I certainly never imagined being a patient on the inside, but I've learned to never say never because anything is possible if we are to be honest with ourselves.

As I walked through the doors of the locked facility I felt as if I had stepped into a lunatic asylum of a century ago where conditions are known to be deplorable and inhumane. The large smoke filled common area was overcrowded and men and women were hollering and acting out aggressively in their cage-like setting. I noticed that the unit was protected by a security officer and wondered if I was in a prison for the criminally insane. My heart ached for these ill and vulnerable patients and at the same time I began to fear for my own personal safety.

One of the major problems of psychiatric hospitalizations is that patients with a wide range of conditions are housed in the same unit so that people with depressive and anxiety disorders are mixed with those that suffer from psychotic disorders like schizophrenia. I can say with certainty that this is a broken system. Depressives absolutely should not be in such an untherapeutic and at times volatile environment.

Within a short time several male patients approached me and made offensive and frightening threats. The security officer walked over to me to chat and then offered advice:

"I'm not a doctor but after speaking with you for a while I know that you don't belong here. I can't help you, but speak to the staff behind the desk and maybe they can assist you."

The security officer provided a little clarity to my confusing and unbearable situation. I took his advice and went to the desk to speak with the staff.

"I was just transferred here from a private psychiatric hospital in Manhattan. I'm here because I suffer from a depressive disorder and I'm certain that I've been placed in the wrong unit."

"That's what everyone feels at first but you do belong here."

I felt like I was in one of those horror flicks that portray a psychiatrist and staff who are unable to distinguish between the sane and insane. I knew that I needed an ally right away so I called my father as soon as I was given the opportunity to make my first telephone call.

"Dad, I think they placed me in a unit for the criminally insane. I need you to do me a favor immediately. Try contacting Dr. D1 at the New York City hospital and let him know where I was transferred today. Ask him to contact the psychiatrists here and inform them that there's been a terrible mistake. "

"Blank, you're probably just anxious about being in a new environment."

"No dad, I don't want to get into specifics, but I don't belong in this place! It's vastly different from the private hospital that I just left. I don't think I'll survive here for too long."

My poor father was probably distressed by my telephone call and I now wish I didn't burden him with my journey through mental illness because he had enough hardships to endure. Sadly it's too late to tell him I'm sorry. My father did come through for me because late that night hospital personnel separated me from the patient population.

"We need to place you in a locked room for the night where you'll feel safe and in the morning you'll be transferred into a different unit of this facility. "

They escorted me to a solitary room and locked me inside. I sat on the floor against a wall in the corner of the room and looked out the observation window feeling like a caged bird that needed to fly and escape all of the hurts of humanity. The following morning I was transferred into a more appropriate section of the facility, but I had lost faith in the center's ability to help in my rehabilitation and I began to develop a defeatist attitude toward psychiatric hospitalizations in general.

Eventually I was discharged, however once I was home I didn't have the knowledge and ability to move forward from the effects of my illness, hospitalizations and psychotropic medications. The trauma from my hospitalizations along with the stigma associated with being an inpatient at a psychiatric facility left me in a more weakened condition than before. My social interactions came to an abrupt end. I was no longer invited to lunch dates or to share in outings to a movie or a day at the beach, so attempts to reengage in past relationships became painful and slowly life as I knew it drifted away.

It was also difficult to find companionship with other psychiatric patients because most of the patients' mental health issues were vastly different from my own. Support groups and group therapy programs can be effective in bringing people together who are facing similar challenges so that they do not feel isolated, however, in the case of mental illness, the issues are too diverse and complex for many individuals to find a common ground.

The issue of how I was coping as a patient inside a psychiatric unit was never discussed with anyone so I attempted to process inconceivable situations on my own, like delusional patients crying out for help at all ends of the corridors, mental health professionals treating patients with disrespect or indifference, and my fears of personal safety during the dark, long nights. Since I lacked the resources to articulate my new trauma I became numb to my feelings and emotions much in the same way that I internalized my mother's chronic illness. This was my minds way of protecting itself from overwhelming experiences. The cost of not addressing the taboo subject of mental illness is that the individual suffers from a lifetime of feelings of shame and severely damaged relationships.

Eventually I met Hillary, a woman with Bipolar disorder. This illness is characterized by extreme mood swings of mania and depression. When we were first introduced she was dealing with episodes of severe depression so we seemed to have a lot in common. Hillary was married to a successful gynecologist, lived in a beautiful home in a prestigious Staten Island community, and appeared to have it all – except mental health. I was not familiar with Bipolar disorder back then so I was completely baffled by Hillary's mood swings. After many months of sharing our experiences with depression, Hillary's mood gradually became elevated. During Hillary's manic episode I tried to cope with her horrendous demands, feelings of grandiosity, and reckless behavior.

Hillary's husband was unable to handle the stress and asked for a divorce, however neither one of them wanted to leave their elaborate house so they literally divided their home into two sections with a rope and when I visited I attempted to stay in neutral territory so that I didn't offend either one of them. I sympathized with Hillary but also understood her husband's dismay because I too was becoming stressed by the relationship. Once the whirlwind of her manic episode passed Hillary went back into a suicidal depression.

One day I received a startling telephone call from Hillary's husband who informed me that Hillary had attempted suicide and was in the emergency room with a stab wound to her chest. He was unable to go to the hospital and asked me to go on his behalf. When I arrived at the hospital an attendant escorted me through long hallways until we arrived at a secured location. He then entered a security code that allowed a door to open into an operating room. I stood frozen as I inadvertently witnessed Hillary's surgery.

"Ms., what are you doing here?"

"Oh no," I responded in a shaken voice. "I was looking for Hillary and was escorted to this room. The hospital staff person must have made a terrible mistake."

I rushed out as quickly as possible and became sick to my stomach by the ghastly scene. Fortunately, Hillary survived her suicide attempt but I realized that I was not strong enough to handle this unstable friendship and made a difficult decision to slowly distance myself from her. I don't know what was more heartbreaking for me – Hillary's Bipolar disorder or the guilt I experienced for letting her down. I came to understand the unpredictable nature of Bipolar disorder, but I was alienating Hillary in the same way that many of the people in my life alienated me.

I was beginning to fear that I was regressing so I began taking trips to Florida to improve my sense of well-being. The sunshine, soft sand, sound of the waves and ocean breeze has always had a calming effect on me. Perhaps I suffer from Seasonal Affective Disorder, a form of depression that most often is encountered in the autumn and winter months when there is little sunlight. My symptoms are slightly improved in the spring and summer even though my depression is major and interminable. Traveling solo was lonely at times, but I found it healing to distance myself physically and mentally from my stressful environment. Once I was receptive to appreciating the beauty of nature I began to reconnect with myself. I usually stayed in a hotel on the west coast near the beach, visiting my childhood friend for dinner from time to time. But travelling is a high-priced luxury and I knew that I needed to return to my family and career. I also realized that it was only a matter of time when the sun would set and my spirit would be darkened once again.

Mr. R. held my position at the law firm for a long period of time but it became evident that I was unable to perform my duties and so I eventually resigned. My depressive disorder combined with my mother's chronic illness was too much to endure so more and more I was becoming less and less. Over the next few years I lived, for the most part, in psychiatric facilities across the New York area and as far as Washington D.C. I realized early on that psychiatric hospitals did not have the resources to provide successful treatment plans for me, but I foolishly believed back then that at the very least these facilities could protect me from myself and my inexplicable desire to self destruct.

During my hospitalizations there were several significant changes in my family. My mother was admitted as a permanent resident at a nursing home at the young age of 57 years old. Initially I was unable to offer emotional support to my mother and father because of my hospitalizations. Also, my brother and his wife became parents of two girls so my extended family was growing.

Through all my hospitalizations I was confused as to whether my admissions were voluntary or involuntary. Most likely, my admissions were all voluntary since I recall hospital personnel insisting that I sign agreements which stated that I was admitted by my own free will. I believe studies demonstrate that a patient who is competent and voluntarily enters a hospital has a better chance of recovery than an individual who is forced; and also voluntary status hinders some of the legal problems that could potentially arise for the hospital. A psychiatrist determines competency of a patient without the protection of a legal hearing and this arrangement has its pros and cons. Make no mistake about the semantics of voluntary admission, once I was on the inside I was under lock and key and powerless in an oppressive environment and requests for discharge were seldom granted.

During my hospitalizations I received invasive treatments like powerful drugs and electric shock therapy and I was never told about the detrimental lifelong consequences. I voluntarily sought assistance for my depression and anxiety, but quite often I was treated with insensitivity. The mental anguish I experienced brings about a somberness which takes my breath away today. I looked for quality care, human connectedness, respect, and hope; but instead fell victim to inferior care, isolation, humiliation and hopelessness.

At times when one particular hospital perceived my behavior to be self destructive they used physical restraints as a safety intervention and treatment plan. The anxiety and shame of being restrained was traumatizing. I sometimes was able to escape the horror by daydreaming, detaching myself physically and mentally from my environment. Detachment was a method that I subconsciously acquired years ago to avoid stressful circumstances. I assume that the staff was supposed to closely monitor me however I was ignored for hours at a time and I was too timid to ask for help even though I was often in physical and mental discomfort. I understand that I was a difficult patient, but why couldn't they devise a less traumatizing treatment plan for me and other patients? I still feel the depth of my humiliation as I write about the experiences even though many years have passed.

All of the hospitals used psychotropic drugs for the treatment of my depression and anxiety, sometimes even overmedicating me. I would say that psychopharmaceuticals is the primary treatment plan for most patients in psychiatric facilities. Nurses do not administer drugs in the privacy of your own hospital room as they do when there is a physical illness; instead I was forced to wait on long medication lines several times a day. Combinations of drugs and high doses of drugs caused horrific symptoms of which I could not set myself free.

My most extreme case of being overmedicated was while I was a patient in a Washington D.C. clinic where each time a drug caused a negative side effect a new drug was added to counteract that side effect until I was taking many powerful drugs at one time. I was supposed to be in the hospital for just a few weeks but I was so physically and mentally impaired that I was unable to travel home alone and remained in the hospital for quite some time before I had the strength to take a flight back to New York City - and the clinic made it evident that I had overstayed my welcome. One evening I staggered out of my hospital room to inform a technician that my migraine headache and dizziness were severe and I needed help. The technician adamantly responded that I was just seeking attention and that I should go back to bed. The problem with asking for help when you have an invisible disease is that everyone believes that you are just seeking attention. The next thing I recall was being awakened by another patient while lying on the floor after fainting. A patient had compassionately laid a pillow beneath my head and sat beside me as she demanded that a doctor be called on my behalf. Once the doctor arrived, he found my blood pressure was dangerously low and was considering transferring me to a medical unit for care. He immediately injected medications and hydrated me and stayed until I was stabilized. How thankful my heart was to be touched by the kindness of these two people. How relieved I was that my symptoms could be identified and treated – and not invisible and profoundly misunderstood.

Despite all of the humiliation, electric shock treatments and adverse reactions from psychotropic medications - the most daunting aspect of my psychiatric hospitalizations was the isolation. I didn't understand the negative attitudes of mental health providers that contributed to patients being isolated, but speculated that it was due to fear, indifference, lack of proper education, or perhaps some loathing of mentally illness. Yet, it seems blatantly evident that every member of the inpatient staff, whether a psychiatrist or a food server, has the potential to have a significant impact on minimizing the isolation of the mentally ill. Early on I understood that I may be received negatively by the hospital staff whether my needs were of vital importance or as basic as respectfully asking for toiletries, so I kept my interactions to a minimum.

"May I use the unit hair dryer?"

"You asked me for the hair dryer yesterday," a female technician responded.

"Yes, but I shower and wash my hair every morning," I said apprehensively.

"I'll give it to you today, but don't ask me again."

These incidents brought about such profound feelings of powerlessness and shame that I felt as if I were going to irretrievably lose my mind in a place that promised to heal it. I began to spend most of the day in my hospital room without stimulation for prolonged periods of time. I was aware of the sounds of patients and staff outside of my door, but meaningful interactions were brief whether I was on the inside or outside of my hospital room. The combination of medications and lack of stimulation significantly warped my sense of time making the minutes, hours and days seem much longer. I felt the isolation thickening in my lungs and suffocating my spirit because socializing is as necessary to survival as the air that we breathe. I obsessively thought about self destruction, not realizing then that my feelings, in part, were a side-effect of isolation. I blamed myself and welcomed the hospitalizations because I didn't think that I belonged on the outside. My hopeless thinking was probably similar to the thoughts of prisoners living in extreme solitary confinement. How can growth, healing, hope or anything good evolve from long-term isolation or loneliness for anyone?

There were occasionally benevolent mental health professionals that I met along the way. I recall one particular technician with a friendly disposition who was willing to take the time to talk with patients. I found myself leaving my room during his shifts and feeling uplifted whenever he was working and I began to notice that there was symptom improvement in other patients as well. As a result of our ordinary conversations about decorating or clothes shopping I felt a little more normal, like it was possible to be on the outside again.

Recently I was in a local store and ran into him for the first time since my hospitalizations years earlier, but I did not recognize him when he called out my name. Later that evening I realized that it was the caring technician and I hope to see him again so that I could express my gratitude for his generosity of spirit during those difficult years. I have a difficult time remembering some of the people that I met during those years because of the invasive treatments for depression I went through. At times memories are completely erased as if certain events had never occurred at all and at other times, if I try hard enough to access events from my past, I can eventually remember a person or incident.

Faced with the challenges of a depressive illness and psychiatric hospitalizations, I'm certain that I would have greatly benefited from more individuals like the technician. Meaningful interactions with staff would have served to remind me that my life had value and that I was not alone. Without adequate support I encountered difficulties reentering society which resulted in repeated hospitalizations.

It is my hope that psychiatrists and psychologists remember their commitment to the following sentence in the Hippocratic Oath and to practice it with love:

"I will remember that there is art to medicine as well as science, and that warmth, sympathy, and understanding may outweigh the surgeon's knife or the chemist's drug."

Reflections on Chapter 11: Inpatient

The reprocessing of the humiliation, sadness, rage and helplessness that I experienced during my hospitalizations reinforced my commitment to telling my story so that I could help raise awareness of some of the issues that affect the mentally ill. Although science still remains at the very early stages of finding cures for mental illnesses I strongly believe that there is hope right now if we can accept and build upon the power of emotional empathy. Perhaps we can begin by asking our educators to place more emphasis on the development of emotional awareness in their students since they will be our future practitioners. Those of us that suffer from mental illness are not a disease – we are unique and valuable individuals who suffer from a disease.

Chapter Twelve

THE FIFTH FLOOR

The nursing home was the final stop on my mother's weary life journey. I can't recall the day my mother was admitted to the nursing home nor can I recall with accuracy the first few years that followed. Electroconvulsive Therapy erased those memories and condemned me to a life of painful speculation. As a consequence, I envision what it was like for my mother to leave her home knowing that all hope for recovery has been exhausted; and I imagine how difficult it was for my father to leave her behind in her new institutional setting among the elderly who for the most part suffer from severe forms of dementia.

My mother resided on the fifth floor of a 300-bed nursing home for the last thirteen years of her life. The nursing home was served by a religious community and was highly recommended by our family physician.

"I'm afraid that you are no longer capable of taking care of your wife at home and a nursing home is necessary. There's a long waiting list at a facility known for excellent care. I'll let the administrators know of your unique circumstances and request that they consider immediate admission."

"Dr. P., my wife is a young woman and a nursing home would be devastating for her. Maybe I can keep her at home a little longer."

"You're no longer able to provide the care that your wife needs. This is a necessary transition which should have taken place years ago. I'm afraid it's time."

Dr. P.'s advice was prudent, the unpredictable nature of multiple sclerosis had taken its toll on my parents physically, emotionally and financially; and my father's health was declining as my mother's needs were increasing. My father's physical health was one of the hidden costs of being a long-term caretaker and perhaps my mental health was the other. At the time my mother was admitted to the nursing home the neurological disorder caused partial paralysis along with other debilitating symptoms that included chronic pain, speech impairment, muscle spasms and blurred vision. As the years advanced my mother became completely paralyzed and totally lost the ability to speak. Multiple sclerosis did not take the transitory course of other catastrophic diseases; instead it incapacitated my mother in small, torturous increments over the course of nearly a lifetime while wearing the life of the primary caretakers.

I can't recall the day my mother was admitted to the nursing home, but I remember the hopelessness of the transition from her home to the nursing home as if it were yesterday. My mother was a relatively young woman with a potentially long life span, yet we still needed to grieve a future that would never be realized. On the day my mother entered the nursing home she suffered the loss of hope for a future; and my father and I lost our freedom as caregivers to the many healthcare providers. My father took upon most of the responsibilities as my mother's caretaker and quickly learned to become my mother's advocate in her new institutional setting, discovering that it was essential to be there as much as possible in order to ensure that my mother's needs were being met. As I'm writing this paragraph and ruminating on my parents' adjustments to the nursing home many years ago, my feelings of guilt and grief are still so visceral that I feel nauseated.

"Blank, I'm on my way to the nursing home."

"There's a blizzard out there. You can't drive."

"I'll walk."

"Dad, it's over a three-mile walk!"

"I know, but your mother will be waiting for me. I have to feed her dinner and make sure they help her to bed properly. You know how short-staffed they are at night. I haven't missed a day in two years and I'm not going to allow a blizzard to stop me."

My father was wholly committed to my mother's care even when she moved to an advanced care facility, neglecting his own well-being. The sudden separation and drastic changes were devastating and my parents had a difficult time accepting defeat. In time, it seemed, my father found his own distinctive way of remaining deeply connected to my mother.

In the earlier years of my mother's admission to the nursing home my battle with depression was severe and I was often in the hospital or respite while psychiatrists tried to regulate my medications; and as a result I was unable to visit the nursing home with routine. Perhaps I subconsciously remained in my own debilitated state because I was unwilling to accept the reality of my family's plight. My weakness of character contributed to their burden and I let them down.

After my stints in the hospitals stabilized I began to visit my mother daily so that I could assist in the facilitation of her care; although at times my visits were merely attempts to relieve my guilt. My father and I would arrive at the nursing home at precisely 4:30 pm so that we could feed my mother her dinner and we stayed until the Nurse's Aides Hoyer lifted my mother into bed sometime after 8:00 pm. I never believed that my nursing home visitation schedule was sufficient and thought I should expend greater efforts in her care. I've always experienced difficulty understanding when enough is enough with respect to almost every aspect of my life – perhaps because my father sacrificed his own well-being for the sake of my mother over the course of a lifetime.

My mother's admission into the nursing home was a despairing period of time in which my mother began to lose her will to live, my father's heart ailment was advancing, and my depression was uncompromising. Some of the challenges we faced were insurmountable as we advocated for necessary services. My mother's new life as a resident of a nursing home was an altered and unchartered landscape of caregiving for us.

My mother was only capable of communicating a few brief words during the early nursing home years and in a barely audible voice she habitually expressed that she wanted to die. Her messages were communicated in a repetitive speech motion which sounded like an involuntary compulsion and was delivered in a rapid rate and a dull tone.

"Your father, your father, your father...."

"But mom, I'm here now. Is that of any comfort to you?"

"I want to die, I want to die, I want to die...."

I became anguished by the fact that I could neither save my mother from her disease nor help her to die.

I began to ponder the question of whether severely handicapped individuals should be granted the right to die. My mother's inability to speak made it impossible for her to engage in conversations with anyone and it was heartbreaking to know that all her feelings were turned inward – incapable of ever being released. I believe that if my mother had the ability to communicate she would have been able to endure her disability because she was an extremely social individual, but instead she remained isolated from human connectedness. Yet despite her limitations, at times, I would notice an innate affability through her tender smiles and expressive eyes which seemed to transcend her isolation.

My mother was one of the youngest residents of the nursing home for a number of years until J. moved to the fifth floor. The first time I noticed J. she was sitting alone in a wheelchair by the nurses' station and I decided to introduce myself. I empathize with the inner struggles of loneliness and I speculated that she was emotionally terrified although it was hidden behind her friendly demeanor. Since I struggle with loneliness I tend to project my feelings unto anyone that I perceive to be isolated. As I approached her I began to shake with fear of being rejected, but I could not evade the potential to help her feel a sense of human connection for just a little while.

"I noticed that you're new here and I just wanted to introduce myself. My mother is a resident on the fifth floor as well and my father and I visit her ever day. I'll introduce you to both of them if you would like."

"I'm J. Excuse my headpiece but I was just listening to a child classical singer, Charlotte Church."

"I'm familiar. I've heard her sing Pie Jesu. She has the voice of an angel."

"I'll ask my husband to make you a copy of the CD."

"No, I wouldn't want to impose on both of you."

"It's not an imposition. I feel better when I'm able to do something for someone."

"Okay, wonderful."

I really didn't want to impose but it seemed to me that accepting J.'s offer would help her to feel needed and I wasn't going to let my pride stand in the way. J. was a woman in her fifties who sustained a spinal cord injury resulting in paralysis of her lower extremities. Her husband was supportive but he was unable to care for her at home. I developed a quick fondness for J. and over time I began to enjoy our brief visits. Typically our conversations were lighthearted but one evening J. shared that she was feeling troubled because the staff didn't always provide relevant information and she felt marginalized. I suggested speaking with a Social Worker but J. seemed too despondent and defeated to explore possible solutions. I was hoping that her upcoming pass to spend the day at home would rejuvenate her spirit. In the meantime, I was considering how I might possibly advocate for her in some small way.

When I visited J. the following day I anticipated our usual temperate conversation, listening with our hearts and responding in gentle tones, but instead she expressed anger toward me.

"Blank, the staff told me that you spoke to them about my feelings of being ignored. I have my own voice and the ability to represent myself when necessary. You had no right to interfere."

Internally I felt as if gentle snowflakes abruptly transformed into an avalanche. Once I processed that I deprived J. of her autonomy my emotions descended rapidly. I was accountable for J.'s distress and I hated myself for my ignorance. I walked away apologetically, but I knew that I needed to do more to repair the damage.

Several days later, as I was standing by my mirror applying makeup, I had a vision of J. serenely smiling at me. Throughout the day I wondered if the unusual image had meaning. Was the image authentic or was my guilty feelings playing mischievous tricks on my mind? Later on I went to the nursing home and looked for J. with the intention of asking for her forgiveness but I couldn't find her anywhere so I made an inquiry at the nurses' station.

"I'm sorry to inform you but J. passed away earlier today. While she was home for the day her husband left her alone to pick up a few groceries and when he returned she was already gone. The cause of death is unknown and there will be no autopsy. The burial is tomorrow and the service is for family only."

I speculated that J. committed suicide in the comfort of her own home surrounded by the things that she valued most in the world. I understood the conditions that would compel her to consider suicide and was despondent about contributing to her grief. Once again I thought about the right-to-die issue for the severely disabled. Living is more than just surviving, I know, but J. was able to communicate and therefore she remained connected to humanity. J. had so much more to give and to receive from this world.

Most likely J., like my mother, did not have the resources that are necessary for a disabled person to feel a sense of well-being and belonging and suicide became the only option. I watched my mother decline when I knew that she would have benefited in a therapeutic environment that concentrated on the needs of multiple sclerosis patients. The nursing home's concentration was primarily on the elderly since younger adults were a minority and severely disabled younger adults have needs that are separate from the elderly. I believe that in addition to their physical disability, the nursing home emotionally crippled my mother and J. and contributed to their hopelessness. I hope that the powerful vision of J. by my mirror was her way of trying to communicate to me that she was finally at peace.

My parents and I often sought social interactions beyond the fifth floor and convened in the reception area after dinner so that we could visit with other residents. Before going to the reception area my father assisted my mother with makeup and jewelry; my mother enjoyed looking presentable despite her illness. Billy Crystal, the comedian, performed a humorous sketch years ago on Saturday Night Live where he repeated a phrase that expressed my mother's spirit: "It is better to look good than to feel good." While my father assisted my mother I often gathered residents in their wheelchairs from various floors and brought them downstairs to the lobby so that we could all be together for a little while. The residents were always eager to share interesting stories of their lives and those who suffered from dementia often told the same stories over and over again.

We met many interesting residents through the years including a woman, Anna, who possessed superb cognitive abilities at the age of 100. Anna kept a diary and recorded all of her activities, even the breakfast, lunch and dinner menu each day. Her hobby appeared pointless to many of the residents until one weekend there was an outbreak of food poisoning and Anna's diary helped the staff to quickly ascertain the cause and treatment of the illness.

There was another resident who suffered from dementia and often attempted to escape from the nursing home in the evenings. She would gather a few fellow-residents and then they would all sneak past the nurse's station managing to make it to the front door of the lobby. Security would then escort the disgruntled ladies back upstairs. My father referred to the resident who orchestrated the excursion as the "ring leader." One evening the ring leader and her followers almost made it out the door when my father swiftly jumped up and approached them.

"Where are you going ladies?"

"We're going to catch the L train to Manhattan."

"It's a cold and rainy night. Maybe you could go to Manhattan tomorrow. I'll escort you to the C train this evening and you'll be greeted by people who will provide a comfortable place to sleep. "

"Thank you, sir. It's been a pleasure meeting you."

My father escorted the ladies to the elevator, pretending it was the C train, and then informed the nurse's station that they were on their way up. Afterwards he chuckled at the scenario even though I was troubled by the offense on their integrity.

"Dad, how could you deceive those poor ladies and then laugh at the situation?"

"Blank, don't take everything so seriously. My intention was to help them and sometimes it's okay to see humor in difficult situations."

From time to time we would socialize with the families of residents in the common areas and our conversations were like group therapy because we were able to commiserate and support one another. As a veteran family of a loved one living in the nursing home, my father and I often shared relevant information to the new concerned family members. Eventually they learned some of the harsh realities of nursing home care through their own personal experiences.

Sometimes people were taken aback by my mother's severe disability and inability to communicate. My father would try to calm their angst using his humor as a tool.

"Just tell me one more thing and I'll leave you alone," my dad would say to my mother spiritedly as the unsuspecting group listened.

"Where did you hide all the money?"

The crowd would inevitably laugh and sometimes my mother would offer an affectionate smile in return.

We often would banter with some of the nuns who worked at the nursing homes as well and they all loved my father's wholesome sense of humor. At times my brother, sister-in-law and two young nieces visited my mother in the lobby of the nursing home and my nieces would entertain us with dance performances which predictably was a crowd pleaser. My mother seldom had visitors and consequently some of the individuals that we met at the nursing became our extended family.

Sr. S., the stern nursing home Administrator, exhibited a rare compassion for my family. One day Sr. S. offered a totally unexpected suggestion.

"Blank, I think you would be a good candidate to become a nun. I could assist you with the process."

"Sister, it's an honor that you would consider me, but I'm afraid that I'm not interested. Besides, I was once married and I've been a sinner on more than one occasion," I said with a grin. Once in a while I exercise a dry sense of humor. I am my father's daughter, after all.

Sr. S. frowned upon large groups congregating in the reception area because she valued quietness, discipline and order. I even witnessed Sr. S. running her finger across the tabletops of the furniture in the lobby to check for dust - perhaps she thought cleanliness is next to godliness. I've always wondered what that adage actually means. Could it be that the religious believe that except for worshiping God, the most important aspect in life is to be clean and orderly? This adage may possibly shed some light as to why my father and I were told that my mother was prohibited from attending mass at the nursing home chapel because her occasional and involuntary groans disrupted the order of the mass. One Christmas, as my father was recuperating in a Manhattan hospital from open heart surgery, my mother and I listened to the holiday service from outside the doors of the chapel, isolated from the community. In the later nursing home years when my father became ill I attempted to keep the routine that he lovingly established.

The holiday season was generally a morose time at the nursing home because many residents were ill or lonely and the more fortunate residents went home to their families, leaving the nursing home eerily quiet. The Salvation Army traditionally donated a small holiday gift to each resident, like stockings or a handkerchief – their gesture touched the spirits of so many. At one time we took my mother home for the holidays but this became too difficult as her illness progressed. So for nearly thirteen years the holiday season was not a time of joyous celebration, but instead a time of reflection and love. I never imagined then that I would come to miss those days.

After the holiday season things would return to normal at the nursing home and our friends would congregate once again in the lobby. We sadly lost many friends along the way because the average lifespan of a resident was about three years. The nursing home was the final place where people went to die and as a consequence standing by the bedside of residents in their final days and attending funerals were routine for me through those years. Some of the bonds established with family of residents were powerful because we shared a common and profound experience. From time to time I have a chance encounter with the family of former residents of the nursing home and even though many years have passed we instinctively embrace as warmth envelopes us. As a result of shared despairing nursing home experiences, a lifetime of connectedness was born.

With the exception of the friendships that we shared and some of the kind-hearted staff that we encountered through those years, the nursing home experience was akin to living in hell on earth. Beyond the pleasant furnishings of the reception area loomed the horrific realities of the fifth floor. It was only a privileged few residents who were well enough to enjoy community friendships and recreational activities. It was more common to see residents curled up in their beds or lined up against the walls of the hallways in their wheelchairs. The Nurse's Aides would sometimes position my mother in the hallway near the fifth floor elevator and when she saw me or my father arrive I noticed an immediate indication of recognition and joy in her eyes. It always broke my heart to see her lined up against the wall with the other residents. In the prime of her life my mother was known for her hopefulness, sophistication and sense of style; then her illness and the nursing home stole the essence of her spirit and dignity.

The environment on the fifth floor was generally noisy and chaotic. Many residents suffered from an agitated form of dementia causing them to repeat cryptic words and phrases over and over again or sometimes they would just scream loudly for no apparent reason. I was especially touched by the elderly who would call out for their mothers or fathers – regressing back to a time when they felt loved and nurtured. I've heard it said that when people exhibit delusional tendencies they should be brought back to reality, however, in the case of the elderly living in nursing homes I don't necessarily agree because the future of this population is grim so why not allow them a moment to escape to a better time. These agitated patients did not respond to drug therapy because they simply needed human connection and love, qualities which are too time intensive and rare to find in a nursing home. Today, though my parents are deceased for many years, I find myself involuntarily calling out their names – perhaps it's a response to my own social isolation.

One of the major problems in the nursing home was that they were always insufficiently staffed which resulted in neglectful and dangerous situations. The nursing home staff were not callous they just generally did not have enough time to attend to all of the personal needs of the residents. When I stopped by the nursing home at random times, for instance, I found that my simple requests were being ignored. I asked that the staff leave my mother's television on her favorite channel during the day because she needed some form of familiarity and stimulation, yet most times her television would be turned off and I would find her alone in her bed staring at the ceiling or situated in her wheelchair facing the walls.

At bedtime, my father and I positioned a call bell near my mother's hands before we left each evening in case she needed assistance even though she did not have the ability to use it – but I guess it helped us to feel a false sense of security.

As a result of the nursing home being insufficiently staffed my mother became prone to bed sores along her spine which could have been alleviated if she was repositioned regularly throughout the day. If she was lying in bed or sitting in a wheelchair for too many hours at a time, the pressure and lack of proper circulation degraded her skin tissue to the point where eventually her bone would appear. At times her bed sores were horrifyingly large and caused a great deal of pain. The process of healing a bed sore was uncomfortable and resulted in her staying in bed on her sides for approximately one month and consistently repositioned from side to side in order to alleviate some of the pressure.

My mother was dependent upon a Hoyer Lift which is mechanical equipment used to lift disabled patients from their wheelchairs and into bed. I recall my mother's primal wails every evening as I waited outside her door for her to be lifted into bed. The Hoyer Lift process required that two Nurse's Aides are present to assist because the consequences of an accident could be catastrophic. As a Hoyer Lift patient there were often extreme delays before she was lifted into bed because the process was time consuming and the aides were busy trying to manage their hectic nighttime rounds. So she waited exhaustedly in pain night after night and when excessive waiting occurred frequently her bed sores would reemerge – it was a vicious cycle.

In her later years her new next door neighbor, C., observed my mother waiting to be placed into bed and generously offered to give up his appointed time so that my mother would be placed into bed each night before him – even though he was fatigued and uncomfortable as well. C. was a gentleman in his 80's who was a retired postal worker, a position that I believe is iconic of American culture, and his persistence represented one of the known attributes of a postal worker.

C. enjoyed outings and visits with his son, daughter-in-law and his grandchildren. When I first met C. his son had recently been elected Surrogate Court Judge and C. proudly exhibited photographs on his nightstand of his son alongside dignitaries, such as former

President Bill Clinton and Hillary Clinton. When my mother passed away, the Judge attended her viewing.

"Judge, we appreciate your visit considering your busy schedule."

"Blank, my father was fond of your family. You all deserve this respect."

Years later I saw the Judge at a local event, but did not feel it was appropriate to approach him because he stood beside prominent community leaders. Instead he quickly walked over to me and hugged me affectionately. Though we live in separate worlds our nursing home experience cemented our connection.

After my mother's passing a number of individuals informed my father and I that we were a quality family who handled our circumstances with dignity, including nuns who taught at an elementary school and high school and shared my father's story as a commendable example of Christian marriage. Yet, I knew in my heart that I did not provide my mother with the emotional support needed from a daughter and so I questioned the validity of their praise.

After a period of painful soul searching I realized that handling my mother's illness with dignity was far from enough. I not only was negligent in providing my mother with appropriate emotional support, but I realized that I would have served my mother more effectively if I consistently advocated for my mother's rights. Unfortunately I was never trained for the important role of caretaker and advocate although I should have instinctually known my responsibilities. It's too bad that the school system does not fully educate us on how to be good parents, children, siblings, friends and finally caretakers and advocates.

The nursing home provided my mother's basic needs but she did not receive necessary physical therapy and recreational therapy, among other things. Consequently, I should have become a fierce advocate. My mother was an advocate for the broken and she deserved the same.

I vividly recall the day my mother died in June 2001. My father and I took my mother downstairs to a small room next to the lobby where we visited our good friends M. and B., relatives of a resident who was in her late 90's and suffered from an extreme form of agitated dementia. Her agitation could be minimized by constant reassurance, an approach which her family devotedly offered with routine. This resident did not act out with anger or aggression but instead her emotions were turned inward; yet through all of her distress there was some remaining vestige of the loving and compassionate woman that she once was.

On this day M. and B. brought their step granddaughter, Emmy, who was approximately four years old at the time. Emmy was absorbing her new environment and seemed to notice something unique to her previous experiences. She must have been wondering why my mother was in a wheelchair and unable to move or speak and perhaps it frightened her. At some point Emmy accepted my mother for her differences and walked over to her and began to smile.

In a heartwarming response, my mother began to smile at Emmy and became unusually responsive to the small crowd in the room. She looked at each of us individually with a radiant smile that suppressed her palpable suffering. I've always found that the smiles of those who are severely ill are the most genuine and profound, a gracious offering when they have so little within them left to give. Perhaps the interaction with an inquisitive little girl kindled my mother's limited ability to connect with her family and friends - one last time.

I then took my mother to her room and I bid her goodnight and hoped I took care of her unexpressed needs. At approximately 3:00 am I received a call from the nursing home and when I answered the phone the nurse placed me on a long hold before conveying the message that my mother had died. As I waited in anticipation for the nurse to return, I heard the sound of a walker in the background, a sound that I heard so many years ago, and I absurdly imagined this eerie sound was my mother walking to the phone to let us know there had been a cure. In reality I was certain that the reversal of her disease was impossible, even my mother lost hope long ago when she asked that I help her die - yet, an element of her once hopefulness survived within me until her very last breath.

I called my brother and sister-in-law to let them know of our mother's passing and to ask my brother to come to the house so that we could both inform my father delicately because he was in a weakened condition as a result of his heart condition. My brother rushed to the house and offered me a supportive hug.

"Louis, we didn't lose our mother today – we lost her gradually and painstakingly over the course of many difficult years."

We informed my father of my mother's passing and then the three of us went to the nursing home to say our final goodbyes. My brother and I gave my father a moment alone with my mother and I overheard his heartfelt words.

"Multiple sclerosis never weakened my love for you. As your disease caused your body to become weaker – my love for you grew stronger."

My brother and I then entered the room. My mother was dressed neatly in a pale blue and white cotton hospital gown with a sheet carefully folded across her lower body and a devotional scapular placed around her neck; the small rectangular cloth bore the following text:

"Whoever dies wearing this scapular shall not suffer eternal fire."

The scapular was given to me, though I now wonder why my mother was not buried with it, and I keep it in my drawer next to a bottle of her favorite perfume – symbolic mementos of my mother's life and death.

I, strangely, spent my time alone with my mother obsessively inspecting her lifeless body because her debilitated body in life appeared very much the same as in death and I could not believe that her suffering was finally over.

One of my mother's regular Nurse's Aide came into the room while I was alone with my mother. I had known this aide for many years and she always appeared to treat my mother with compassion.

"She died in her sleep, Blank. We did our nightly rounds to check on her and she was already gone."

I was so sad that my mother died alone and wondered if she struggled while unable to call out for help – it was always my fear that she would die in this way. Then without processing my thoughts I asked the aide the unthinkable.

"Blank, how could you say that! Maybe I misunderstood what you just said."

"I want to know if my mother suffered an accidental fall tonight. I'm wondering why I left my mother only hours ago in wonderfully good spirits and now she's lying here deceased – with a bruised eye."

Reflections on Chapter 12: The Fifth Floor

Despite the passage of time since my mother's passing my pervasive feelings continue to be sadness for all of my mother's suffering and unbearable remorse for not providing her with greater care at home and through the nursing home years. Remorse is especially difficult when it is far too late to make things right.

Nevertheless, I am weary of the stagnation of my self-resentment and I'm trying to find a way to forgive myself. Forgiveness begins by understanding why the transgression occurred in the first place and the writing of my book, particularly this chapter, helped me to see various perspectives of the truth of my past. I discovered that multiple sclerosis is a disease that affects the emotions and behavior of the entire family. Over time each of my family members developed their own method of encountering the unpredictable storm. My response was a combination of avoidance and hostility, behaviors that were developed, at least in part, to protect myself from emotional pain. Until recently it was difficult for me to acknowledge my personal struggles because they paled in comparison to the struggles of my poor mother.

It is my hope that families of individuals with multiple sclerosis seek professional support because I believe that therapeutic intervention would have helped my family and quite possibly my emerging depression. Knowing that I did not have the proper support back then helps me to find some forgiveness today, however, the reality is that forgiveness is sometimes not a permanent state of mind as it tends to be strong in one moment and weak in the next. It also helps to remember the gentle smile that my mother offered to everyone around her on the day she died. Smiling through pain is a beautiful gift of love.

Chapter Thirteen

AN UNCOMMON BOND

One of my childhood obsessions was to watch television shows that depicted the traditional American family, like the Brady Bunch. As I sat on the floor in my bedroom staring into my black and white television I felt despondent that my family was not as ideal as the television families, that they struggled with incomprehensible adversity, that my father was cast in the conventional role of financial provider as well as the unconventional role of housekeeper and caregiver. In spite of my mother's declining health she held sovereign claim on our family, but when she was too ill to provide nurturance my father even went beyond the household chores and attempted to boost our spirits. I recall an uplifting incident when I was a bored seven-year old.

"Dad, I didn't have friends to play with today and I'm feeling very bored."

"How about I teach you how to play the card game, War?"

"Wow, really?"

"It's simple and if you're lucky you can win all the cards!"

As we competed in the game of War my cheerless mood was totally transformed. I've played this heartwarming moment in my head a million times, dad smiling with a deck of cards in his hands at our round wooden kitchen table. With inexhaustible patience my father managed the special challenges of working, cleaning, cooking, laundry, caring for my mother, and at times meeting our emotional needs. My father innately knew how to embrace his difficult journey; his emotional strength is his legacy.

My relationship with my father went through many changes; our final chapter presented the most significant challenges. After my hospitalizations I lived alone with my father for seventeen years in a relationship that appeared to be regressing rather than evolving because we remained stuck in a parent-child relationship. One of the obstacles was my inability to live independently and another was the tension of caring for my mother during the nursing home years. My father and I established many of the same roles that are found in traditional marriages, like sharing grocery shopping, cleaning and companionship at social functions. Very often it seemed as if all we had left in the world was each other. Nevertheless, our intense bond was an unnatural bond and the stress involved in the absence of what is natural and central to being human in today's American culture hurt our relationship - opening up, for me, subconscious wounds from the past. Despite our challenges, I think we both knew that we loved one another. If only I could have let go of all of my defenses and told him so. If I could have one lifetime wish – I would ask for one more conversation with my father.

It is difficult to grasp that many years have passed since the sole thread that joined me to a nuclear family perished. On March 15, 2006, my brother and I made the difficult decision, under the advice and supervision of physicians, to increase his morphine during the night even though premature death was a likely consequence.

"Louis, dad will die because of our choices. Shouldn't we continue to hope that he'll be stabilized and we could all be together for a little while longer?"

"Blank, the doctors are unable to control the pain from his cancer. We should pray that God will take him and end his suffering."

There are moments in life when a situation is so harrowing that we can't begin to fathom what to hope or pray for because we know in our heart that every realistic outcome is grave. Once the lethal decision was made I regressed into a shadowy state of denial.

When I arrived at the hospital the following evening the doctors informed me that he most likely would not survive through the night. At this juncture I should have not moved from his bedside, reassured him, stroked him and expressed my love and gratitude to him - but I did not. It was my intention to stay with him through the night but for some reason, after I spoke with his doctor, I took a leisurely stroll through the large New York City hospital and slowly and methodically sifted through the hospital snack shop. I can't recall what was on my mind exactly but it felt as if there was a veil between me and reality and my obscure thought processes allowed me to believe that his imminent death would wait for me. It was as if I thought that I could hit the pause button on life and his death would come to a halt until I was prepared.

I somberly walked back to my father's hospital room with a vague sense that something deeply critical was looming. I rested on a large chair beside his bed and placed my hot coffee on the food tray, feeling a chill as the warmth slipped away from my fingertips. My brother was on his cell phone speaking with our cousin on the opposite side of the room. As my father laid asleep the gurgling sound of his labored breathing, or the death rattle as I now realize the process is known, filled the room with hopeless unrest. Only a brief time passed when the rattling sound abruptly ceased. Just as animals have an instinct to foresee imminent natural catastrophes, as was widely noted in the tsunami in Asia in 2004, I instinctively knew that a powerful life force was now in control and it was far too late to escape the rising tide.

The next few moments unfolded in slow motion and reality appeared to be strikingly impenetrable. I rose from my chair and stood by his bedside helplessly watching as he pulled his head up and gasped for air. I should have comforted him but I was trapped in another perceptual world and the powerful life force would not pause for me any longer. His fearful and glassy eyes caught mine and death overcame him.

I looked up at the clock and mentally noted that the time of his death was 10:50 pm. Perhaps it's common to glance at a clock at the time of death of a loved one because we need to create a visual representation of the intangible nature of the moment of the passing of human life. It seemed that at 10:50 pm I also lost my sense of self with the person that I loved most in this world. With the passing of my mother five years earlier and now the passing of my father I

154

immediately felt like an adult orphan. I walked out of the room in a daze, my eyes peering down the hallway toward the nurse's station, and hesitantly muttered words that even today seem surreal:

"Nurse - my father just passed away."

My life closed twice before its close;
It yet remains to see
If Immortality unveil
A third event to me,
So huge, so hopeless to conceive,
As these that twice befell.
Parting is all we know of heaven,
And all we need of hell. (Emily Dickinson)

We all know that with each breath we take we are closer to our last and yet we are always unprepared for the inevitable. As I watched my father's still body I was overwhelmed with love and I could not fully fathom that he was gone. My father witnessed my first breath and I witnessed his last – the cycle of life ends in a tragedy.

The following day I asked my brother to meet me at my father's house so that I could collect his burial garments. As I moved through my father's bedroom I could sense his presence. I clutched his clothing securely next to my heart as if I were gripping and grasping my inconsolable grief. As I glanced toward my father's bed I noticed something that seemed spiritual or inexplicably mysterious.

"Hurry into dad's room," I shouted.

"Blank, what's wrong?"

"Look," I said, as I pointed towards my father's bed.

My brother and I stood aghast as we observed that the clock on my father's nightstand stood still at the precise time of his death and that a portrait of our mother had fallen from the wall and was positioned beside his nightstand. We attempted to make sense of what appeared to be a message without words, but our grief was raw and making sense of the world without my father was beyond words. We eventually theorized that my father was trying to communicate that he passed from his earthly existence into a realm where time is infinite and that he was reunited with my mother. I wish, however, I could firmly believe that there is life after death. Since that experience I have never again felt my father's energy although I call to him in times of despair.

While I was driving alone to his wake and funeral over the next few days I was struck by the painful void of his life – no rushing to emergency rooms, no conversations, no human connection, nothing today and nothing tomorrow. My grief literally slowed down my breathing as well as my visual and auditory perceptions, as if I were driving while intoxicated. I kept wishing, oddly, that my father could somehow be with me to help me through my fears and bereavement.

The first few days after the funeral I would appear at my brother's door step, uninvited. The two of us sat on his porch trying to come to terms with the cataclysm in our lives and our strange new sense of self after the loss of our father. I don't remember the condolences from friends and family at the funeral - I only remember their silence in the weeks and months that followed. Not long ago my friend's father passed away and I visited her while she was sitting Shiva. In Judaism, Shiva is a seven-day mourning period for the immediate family of the deceased during which friends and family gather in the home of the bereaved to offer comfort food and support. It appeared to be emotionally healing for her and I could not help but contemplate on the contrast in my own life and religion.

Within a few days of my father's death I returned to work but I did not share my grief with co-workers because most people couldn't understand the uncommon bond with my father. Both my unusual grief and my battles with depression were so painfully abstruse that it is difficult for most people to understand the depth of those feelings.

Grieving alone was perhaps the most dangerous and isolating human experience I have ever known and since then I am resolved not to let anyone I care about grieve alone. I usually try to hide my sorrow when I am in public, as my parents once did, despite the fact that I subconsciously wear my depression on my sleeve. It has always seemed that hiding sorrow is necessary in order to maintain relationships with the people that exist on the periphery of my world. There is a renowned poem by Ella Wheeler Wilcox entitled "Solitude," which reads, "Laugh, and the world laughs with you; weep, and you weep alone."

After my father's death, I immediately felt an extraordinary failing in my purpose in life and I could not even envision ever returning to a balanced existence because I never knew a normal way of living and functioning. I was not a mother, wife or caretaker and now I would never again be a daughter. With the absence of my father there would be no one to support me today, no one tomorrow - and no one to glance at the clock at the hour of my death. The perception of life that was cultivated through my persistent battles with depression was now fortified with unrecoverable grief.

I was also physically and emotionally exhausted from the long and stressful period of caring for my father. The grief of a long-term caregiver is also unlike other forms of grief. While travelling the rollercoaster of heart disease and cancer I struggled with anticipatory grief, envisioning my life without my father over and over again. The last few months of my father's life were besieged with agonizing and perplexing health issues that included bloody sputum, shortness of breath, a hoarse voice, fatigue and pain. My father and I went back and forth to hospital emergency rooms, struggling with every step and every breath, as he was erroneously treated for a pre-existing heart disease and released. Once an individual has a pre-existing condition it appears to be difficult for healthcare providers to think outside the box when new symptoms arise and so upon each visit the elephant in the room was ignored. One of his last admissions was for the insertion of a defibrillator and he was released from the hospital only twenty four hours after the procedure. Within hours of his release from the hospital he had a massive heart attack. The insertion of a defibrillator was drastically invasive and outrageously needless for an individual with end stage lung cancer. I also speculate that the cancer began to rapidly metastasize as a direct result of the procedure because within weeks his cough became increasingly persistent, his voice was significantly weaker, and his fatigue and pain were profoundly intensified.

Finally, on February 14, 2006, my father was informed that he most likely was suffering from end stage lung cancer, approximately one week later these findings were confirmed through a lung biopsy, and on March 16, 2006 he passed away. Sadly he spent most of his final days in doctors' offices and emergency rooms being treated for heart disease rather than being managed by oncologists or hospice, practitioners who could have addressed his physical and emotional needs. When an individual is suffering at the end of their life every second is precious.

After my father's cancer diagnosis he spent a few days in a Staten Island hospital where his needs continued to be grossly unsatisfied. My brother and I decided that he would receive better care in a New York City hospital and we requested a transfer, however the transfer was denied by the attending pulmonary physician and my father's insurance company.

Consequently, in our desperate hours, my brother and I plotted to abduct and rescue my father from the hospital in Staten Island and bring him to one of the New York City hospitals. This was a complicated maneuver and the dramatic scenario unfolded with the grandiosity of a theatrical event. First I informed the attending pulmonary doctor that I intended to transfer my father to another hospital despite his professional recommendations; and I requested that he surrender all of my father's medical reports including X-rays and MRI scans. He informed me that they could be found at a diagnostic imaging facility however when I arrived at the facility, directly after our conversation, I discovered that the pulmonary physician seized the images only minutes before. I then became guarded about the coincidental timing and began to look over my shoulders as my brother and I planned our next steps. My brother and sister-in-law rose to the occasion when the final crisis hit while I fell short in my father's final days, perhaps because of my exhaustion from helping him with his care for so many years.

We hired a private ambulance who agreed in advance to help us transport my father with the stipulation that we would pay their fee in cash because they didn't want a paper trail since they were concerned that we were transporting our father without the proper release or transfer forms. My sister-in-law waited outside the hospital for the ambulance and informed us when it arrived. My brother and I then assisted my father from his hospital bed into a wheelchair and we swiftly escaped the unit as the nurses called for security in an attempt to stop us. Despite the commotion we managed to rush my father through the long corridors and out the front hospital doors. The ambulance personnel met us by the curbside of the hospital where my father was quickly lifted onto a gurney and into the ambulance while I jumped in behind him so that I could be by his side. My brother and sister-in-law followed the ambulance in their car as we took the long ride to New York City.

"Dad, I know you're uncomfortable, but in a little while you'll receive the care that you deserve."

My father was in pain and coughing violently however he did not protest our last attempt to help him because I believe that he appreciated being rescued and was beginning to feel a glimmer of hope that things could improve. I could hardly breathe along the way because I feared that the police would stop us, but I began to feel confident when we exited the Brooklyn Battery Tunnel and entered New York City.

The moment we walked into the doors of the emergency room of the New York City hospital we knew that the facility offered the highest level of care. The contrast between the two hospitals was so evident that it appeared as if we had left a third world country hospital and arrived at a hospital in a highly developed society. The environment was astonishingly sophisticated with highly technical innovations and comfortable accommodations. Our leap of faith into this remarkable world of quality healthcare was proving to be promising, but when the admitting doctor considered denying my father admission because of our peculiar circumstances we realized that our plan was fallible. As we attempted to explain how it came to be that we arrived at the doors of their hospital it occurred to us for the first time that our situation was indeed outlandish.

"You must understand that it's unprecedented that a patient would be transported from another hospital by ambulance without a formal process."

Well, maybe, but we know that this is one of the best hospitals in the world and we need your help. My father wasn't treated with the dignity that he deserved at the hospital in Staten Island."

"You're certainly making an intriguing argument. Your father is being stabilized and I'm going to have a team meeting with the other physicians so that we could discuss your unusual circumstances."

My brother, sister-in-law and I anxiously waited for the hospital to render a decision and in those hours my father was beginning to gain strength. The extraordinary doctors were able to hydrate, feed and administer appropriate levels of morphine and for the first time in months my father appeared to be comfortable.

The physicians decided to admit my father although they had little options given his grave condition.

"Thank you," I said. "Perhaps you can't cure my father but I know that you could help him die with dignity."

As the weeks progressed the team of doctors became extremely fond of my father. They referred to him as a "quality gentlemen" and enjoyed his wisdom and gentle sense of humor.

One evening I received a wonderfully perplexing telephone call from the physicians.

"Blank, we have a splendid surprise for you, but your father would like to come to the telephone and tell you personally."

I could hear joyful outbursts from a group of people in the background but I was baffled because my father's voice was barely audible for quite some time, and he was a patient in a hospital unit where laughter was seldom heard. I waited, apprehensively, for someone to return to the telephone to explain.

"It's dad," my father said in his old familiar voice.

"Dad?"

"Yes," he said elatedly. I'm still in the operating room and I'm celebrating with my friends who perform miracles. The surgeons were able to move the tumor that was pressing against my vocal cord and I can speak again! It was actually a painless procedure."

"After all this time you have your voice back again? Dad, those surgeons gave you something so immensely valuable."

With sorrowful disappointment to everyone who cared for my father he had a stroke only a few days later which took away his mobility, voice and spirit.

"I'll see you the day after tomorrow Mr. C.," my father's doctor said.

With his warm smiling eyes he mouthed the words: "I will not be here."

His doctor walked away with a tear running down her cheek and two days later my father passed away. The compassion that the doctor showed to my father was beyond anything that I had ever witnessed among healthcare professionals and my gratitude still runs deep. There is no greater gift than when we are recipients of profound compassion. Years after my father's passing I made an unsuccessful attempt to obtain the doctor's contact information so that I could let her know that her gift still lives on within my heart.

Reflections on Chapter 13: An Uncommon Bond

As a depressive and an individual without a family of my own the loss of my father has been insufferable and I know that the sorrow and the longing for the unconditional love of a parent will echo within my heart until my own death. And, as with my mother, I am left with agonizing remorse for all of my negative emotions during his living years. Shortly after my father's passing I began grieving the loss of two father figures when my therapist suddenly abandoned his practice.

As I reflected on this chapter I wanted to offer hope to depressives and their parents, therapists, siblings and friends who are dealing with difficult emotions in their relationships so that they will not suffer my fate. The negative emotions of a depressive affect not only the individual, but everyone who cares for the depressive. If relationship issues remain unaddressed, sooner or later the relationship will suffer damages that are impossible to remedy. However, it is possible to lessen some of the negativity if we are willing to open up our hearts and share our thoughts and feelings. Hope is a verb that requires some type of action. I am certain that my father and I would have had a better relationship if we engaged in empathetic communication; and I believe that if my former therapist and I were able to effectively communicate things would not have gone cataclysmically awry.

Effective communication, a skill that can be developed with the support of a therapist, life coach or self-help books, fosters warmth and trust in every relationship and it is especially helpful in the case of depressives who are overwhelmed with persistent feelings of doubt and fear. It is possible to make something beautiful out of struggles; furthermore, the heavy burden of remorse will be lifted if we know in our hearts that we at least tried to make a difference. We all suffer from the damages of our past, but the important thing is to recognize what we are doing wrong and then try our best to rise above it and make it right.

Chapter Fourteen

WILLIAM

At one time I measured the quality of a person's character by their achievements in higher education, career and financial strength rather than the essence of their humanity. So when I found myself unemployed as a result of my psychological disability after my first hospitalization I was riddled with internal judgment. My feelings of inadequacy began to snowball, increasing in size and intensity with each passing day. As the days turned into months, months turned into years, and years turned into a decade the probability that I would return to work became increasingly doubtful. My inability to be mentally challenged at work, the loss of structure and the loss of peer interactions understandably exasperated my depression. The negativity in my life just kept snowballing until I was trapped and suffocating inside a full-blown avalanche.

My symptoms became immobilizing, making it seem impossible to leave the house to do things that were once pleasurable. I buried myself in my room to avoid the light of day, like a worm pushing its way further and further into the darkness of the soft earth. I yearned for someone to reach deep inside the darkness and touch my soul because I knew that recovery would not come from an oval blue pill or another hospitalization.

Sometimes I fantasized about feeling better and returning to work. Positive visualization allowed me to replace thoughts of failure with thoughts of success in a career and new friendships. In those moments of escape I didn't worry about how my depressive symptoms would interfere with interviews and assigned workloads, I just imagined myself immersed in meaningful work or enjoying conversations with peers around a water cooler. At a certain point I accepted that I was not getting better and considered the possibility of working with a major depressive illness because if I did nothing at all my life would remain the same. After a decade of unemployment had passed I began the difficult journey from isolation to inclusion with the help of Dr. D. The catalyst for change begins with imagination, then hope, then action.

I decided to hide my past from potential employers because I already lost so much as a result of stigma. I would like to imagine a world where there is greater support for those who are ill and trying to reenter the workforce, but the reality is that employers need to trust that they are hiring someone who is fully capable of fulfilling the requirements of the job. After months of rigorously searching for a part-time office position, I concluded that I was no longer qualified because of all of the advances in technology as well as my outright lack of ability to self-market. I was grateful when I was finally offered a position in a small after-school program monitoring kindergarteners through sixth graders two hours a day in the winter of 2000.

My anxiety assuredly took a life of its own when I first looked into the eyes of seven high spirited kindergarteners. I wanted to take a moment to work through my fears but one of the children waived her hand persistently in the air before I had a chance.

"Umm, do you want to say something?"

"Yep, I'm Amy and I'm the pencil sharpener monitor!"

Although I didn't have any prior training I had a gut feeling that I needed to quickly take control of this situation or these children would take control of the classroom.

"Well, Amy, I want you to know that I take the job of monitoring pencils very seriously. You must first learn the skill for sharpening pencils and creating a perfect point. Plus, as pencil sharpener monitor, you need to be sure that you do this safely and that all of your classmates' pencils are perfectly pointed too. I'll show you how and if you can prove to me that you could be a good pencil sharpener monitor by the end of the week you have the job."

Surprisingly my impromptu psychological experiment worked and I took command of the kindergarten classroom which helped me to build confidence for my next assignment. One afternoon Mr. Y., the owner and principal of the after-school program, requested that I work with the sixth graders in the Hunter program. The program was designed to prepare students for the entrance exam for the Hunter College School, one of the most sought after schools in New York City. Even though Mr. Y. was the principal, the Hunter program children predominated, and as a consequence their dislike for their teacher caused her to be permanently removed and their fondness for me secured a position in which I was not trained to handle. It was my impression that Mr. Y. did not always weigh whether his decisions were in the best interest of the children in his program. In my reentrance into society I was beginning to notice that I was often saner than those that are considered mentally competent.

"Mr. Y., please relieve me of my responsibilities with the Hunter children. They only have a few weeks before their exam and they deserve a licensed and trained teacher."

"Blank, they like you and that will help them as they prepare for the exam. Just be sure that the students complete the sample test questions that I'll provide each day and they'll be fine."

It was difficult to accept that the Hunter children liked me although I yearned to believe that it was true because I needed to fill the empty, aching feeling in my heart. I decided to put my emotions aside and remain focused and objective because what these children needed most was an effective environment where they could study for their exam. But when one of the children gave me his art during the holiday season I felt the tears swell in my eyes. His penciled sketch of a decorated Christmas tree beside a lit menorah is now safely tucked away in my keepsake box.

Despite my feelings to the contrary, Mr. Y. determined that the remainder of my assignment would be to work solely with the Hunter program students. So each day I administered sample tests and after grading their tests I found that the students were remarkably gifted in math and science. However, since my class consisted of children of Korean-born immigrants, they struggled with English and essay writing. The most gifted child, William, scored astonishingly well on all of the tests but he repeatedly refused to write the required simple essay. I decided to intervene even though I was intimidated by William's unordinary intelligence and his predisposition to fits of rage.

"William, I would like to try and help you with your essays after class."

"I don't need your help!"

"I think you need help from someone and it seems that I may be the only person offering. If you want to have a chance to succeed on the Hunter exam then let me help you."

"Is someone giving you extra money to help me?"

"That should not be your concern, William. I was given permission for you to stay after class today and over the next couple of weeks. Let's begin by writing down a few ideas for the subject of your essay."

While William was considering subjects for his essay I was becoming more and more anxious and concerned. I promised William that I would help him but I didn't know what approach would be the most constructive. All that I could remember from my elementary school writing class was that an essay must include an introduction, body and conclusion and I prayed that this simple framework would somehow help him.

"William, why aren't you writing down topics for your essay?"

"Is my father or Mr. Y. paying you to help me?"

"It's not proper for you to repeatedly ask questions about my salary."

"Please answer me, Miss Blank."

"Okay, I think you need to know the truth about my salary because for whatever reason it seems to make a difference to you. I am not getting paid to help you. You're young but very bright so I think you'll understand what I'm about to tell you. Well, you see...I haven't really done too many nice things in my life, those kinds of things that could make a difference. I will feel better about myself by doing something nice for someone else - so by helping you I'm really helping myself. Now, will you let me help you William?"

Fortunately this was the response that William needed to hear and he allowed me to help him. It struck me that despite the vast differences in our age and culture, William and I shared similar fears that were holding us back. William was also besieged with fears of being judged and he was probably trying to protect himself from further feelings of shame. I knew in my heart that William needed to find acceptance and support so that he could begin to believe in himself.

"I tried but I can't write an essay!"

"William, stop thinking about your limitations and start imagining that with my help you could do it. Imagination could be an important first step in tackling your fear of writing. I know it sounds silly, but this kind of trickery of the mind recently worked for me so let's give it a try."

William began to fantasize about writing an essay, passing the test and being accepted in the Hunter program. William's positive thinking eventually helped him to take a chance and practice writing. I recall William's expression of jubilance when he finally caught on and it was by far one of the most rewarding experiences in my life - and may very well be the spark which ignited a hunger in me to more fully immerse myself in my radically interrupted life. By helping

William I recognized my inner strength and my ability to make contributions to society, and I gained the self esteem necessary to seek other employment opportunities once the after-school program ended. I hope my spark kindled a soft flame in William too.

I would like to be in a position to advocate for employment opportunities for individuals with mental illnesses so that I can help someone else recognize their inner strength and gain confidence, however without the proper education I have been unable to find an appropriate forum. I believe that we can help individuals with mental illnesses find and maintain jobs if we educate employers and employees on negotiating common problems in the workplace, like slight adjustments that need to be made in the work environment as well as addressing the problems of stigma. Every individual, including those with disabilities, possesses talents that could be beneficial to employers given the appropriate environment; and every individual needs to believe that they are a contributing member of society.

Several months after working at the after school program, I began working a few hours a week for a cultural center where I assisted with tours, among other things. As I gradually increased my responsibilities I gained confidence in my ability to be meaningfully employed. Although each day presented significant obstacles I found ways to incorporate some balance, like limiting my hours in the workplace.

In 2004, I rejoined the corporate workforce as a part-time office assistant at a local organization. The experience was daunting because I was forced to recognize my incompetence in an environment where I once excelled. As time progressed I was able to contribute

171

more but it took years before I was given the opportunity to step outside of my entry level role. In the meantime, I became frustrated and dismayed because I needed to work harder than most people to achieve goals and to be recognized. It was a damaging experience to be deprived of the opportunity to contribute some of my skills for so long. I took a leap of faith when I reentered the workforce, but I needed my employers to see my value and help me with the next baby step into meaningful work.

While I was trying to maintain my job in the organization I was enduring numerous difficulties in my personal life, including my father's death in 2006. There were days when I thought I would need to leave my job because the stress was exasperating the symptoms of my depressive disorder, however, after the loss of my father I needed the extra income to survive. And, most importantly, I was determined to never give up because it was an unbearable struggle to return to mainstream and I never want to lose my footing again.

It took a number of years before the stress of working became normal and endurable stress, but I still needed to maintain a more steady balance. When my emotional issues became so intrusive that I could not concentrate, I attempted to converse with co-workers who had downtime and then took my work home to make up for lost time. At a certain point I was able to take a step back and look at my employment in a positive light, realizing that my reentrance into the workforce brought pride and normalcy in a life plagued by chronic depression. I began to truly care about the organization and the well-being of my co-workers. I was extraordinarily thankful that many of my co-workers were a part of my life and I sometimes wished that I could share my story and let them know just how much they meant to me – but how could anyone even begin to understand?

In 2012, eight years after I was hired, I was offered my long-awaited lateral promotion as Membership Liaison and then the following year I became an Event Coordinator with the responsibility of coordinating both small and large scale corporate events. CC, the President of the organization, and my supervisors AP and JG looked beyond my weaknesses and recognized strengths that I did not see in myself and over time their perspectives helped me to positively assess my contributions to the organization. In 2013, I was one of thirty-one women who were presented with a New York City Council Citation and Women of Influence Award for personal achievements in career.

I still can't free myself from negative self-judgment, but I am not as hard on myself as I was during my years of unemployment because I also judge myself on my perseverance and my ability to transform my employment fantasy into a reality. I defy contemporary thinking by redefining success as the ability to be resilient in the face of adversity. While my peers were building their lives, I learned with every fiber of my being about caretaking, human struggle and compassion and I believe my life experience gives me a fundamental right to be worthy of the same dignity, respect and opportunities as those who are successful in higher education and career.

Even though my depressive illness, with all of it impossibly massive sensitivities, makes it difficult to get through the workday I learned to fight through my struggles and move forward. Every day is about finding enough courage and determination to accept myself and to remain connected to life and all of its joys and sorrows.

Whenever my employment issues beckon the demons in my head I'm encouraged by the infamous words of Sir Winston Churchill: "...never; never; never; never – in nothing great or small, large or petty – never give in except to convictions of honor and good sense."

Reflections on Chapter 14: William

I dedicated this chapter to William, a young boy on the fringe of my small circle, who provided a needed sense of fulfillment well over a decade ago. I can still visualize William sitting at his desk bearing an expression of mistrust in his intensely competitive educational environment. Once William began to have faith in me our brief relationship proved to be one of the most gratifying experiences of my life, and it helped me to reengage in employment and ultimately a life that was brutally interrupted by my battles with depression. It is often the case that individuals and circumstances that exist in the outermost edges of our lives bring opportunities for transformation that would have otherwise not been possible.

It was painfully difficult for me to reintegrate into the workforce because of a stigma of mental illness, among other things. There are laws that prohibit discrimination of qualified individuals with disabilities but the truth remains that employers will find their way around established laws. Still, employment has been vital to my psychological and financial well-being despite the many challenges. I strongly encourage individuals struggling with anxiety and depression to find and/or remain meaningfully employed because the daily structure and social affiliations will help you reclaim your life.

Chapter Fifteen

THERAPY

It's all a blur, but without a doubt, my long-term treatment for chronic depression began when I decided to seek professional help with my relationship with my former husband prior to our wedding in 1989. I never spoke with a psychologist before that period of time, but it's my longstanding modus operandi to seek advice when the unutterable answer already exists deep within my heart and is struggling to be heard. I knew very little about the therapeutic process, but hoped that an analyst had the ability to make sense of my fiancé's chaotic behavior and provide a treatment plan that would bring about therapeutic change in merely one or two sessions. I felt certain that I would not be committing to the long-term variety of psychoanalysis where a patient lies on a couch and free associates in order to discover the origins of their inmost anxieties.

"I've given you a brief background of my life. Can you advise me on how to better handle my conflict-ridden relationship with my fiancé before my wedding day?" I asked apprehensively.

"Blank, your fiancé doesn't love you and he's emotionally abusive. My advice is to cancel the wedding immediately and I'd like to see you twice weekly for long-term treatment for - *depression.*"

Diane's bombshell revelations were too painful to fully accept because they rocked my sense of identity, so I went into my usual denial mode and insisted that her opinions were fraught with error despite all the obvious evidence.

"Diane, my fiancée cares about me and I'm not going to cancel the wedding. Furthermore, I'm not depressed! It's my mother who suffers from depression from time to time. When I was a child I lived with extended family when her bouts with depression were so severe that she was unable to care for me. She has multiple sclerosis and understandably becomes depressed every now and then; whereas I have absolutely no right to be depressed. I'm here today because I want advice on how to help my fiancé with his issues."

There were times when I doubted my fiancé's love for me but I never so much as dabbled with the concept of my own depression. I was acutely aware of my profound sense of aloneness, as if I was separated by time and distance from the rest of the world, but I didn't understand that I may have been suffering from a disorder. The main concern of my family was my mother's illness, although in hindsight I realize that the other problems hid in the shadows patiently waiting for their big reveal. I should have questioned my feelings of aloneness, but I didn't have the emotional maturity to look deep within my heart; and I should have questioned Diane's assessments more thoroughly, but I wasn't confident enough to question authority and I wasn't wise enough to accept good advice - so I bolted from her office as swiftly as a cheetah running at full speed.

Diane was perceptive and in hindsight I realize that she was a skillful therapist. It was courageous of her to render life-changing recommendations and a diagnosis in just one session, although she probably acted expeditiously because she realized that time was not on my side. Diane listened to me at a level which was beyond rudimentary, quickly identifying issues that were unstated. She even followed-up with me on a number of occasions to request that I reconsider entering into a therapeutic relationship, but it wasn't until years later that I realized that her level of concern was a rare quality in a therapist and it was a devastating decision not to heed her advice.

Shortly after my wedding day I knew that I needed to explore anti-anxiety medications to help me cope with the challenges of my ill-fated marriage. Diane was unquestionably the catalyst for my looking inward, however a psychologist doesn't have prescribing privileges so I searched the yellow pages for a psychiatrist and that's how I found Dr. S. I did not research Dr. S.'s credentials because I was a novice consumer at that time. It behooves the mental health consumer to spend some time assessing a provider's capabilities because of the emotional investment of forming a trusting relationship as well as the financial investment.

This should have been a period of time to learn from my mistakes and move forward but instead I retreated. Finding solutions to my problems, whether large or small, has always been a crippling affair because I tend to focus my full energy on the problem rather than the solution. At this particular time in my life it became increasingly difficult to carry my burdens so the negligible addition of my marital woes caused me to spiral into a repugnant murky pit.

Dr. S. recommended my first psychiatric hospitalization and I was feeling so exhausted and confused that I surrendered to his authority without any understanding of a treatment plan. Once inside I was frightened about trusting strangers with my well-being while Dr. S. was so far out of reach. My misery accumulated when Dr. S. contacted me at the hospital to let me know he was dismissing me as his patient. From then on I feared abandonment with all my therapists and eventually my fears became a self-fulfilling prophecy.

As I lay in my hospital bed gazing at the sterile and barren environment, isolated from everything and everyone I had ever known, I made a conscious decision to implement a strategy that would present the greatest danger to my depression – I decided to give up. I was exhausted and no longer wanted to contend with my challenges and decided to literally disengage from almost every aspect of life. I've always wanted to leave the world a better place in some small way, yet at this particular time I believed there was absolutely no hope that I would be able to contribute anything of value to anyone.

From as far back as I could remember I isolated my emotions into distinct and separate parts so that, for example, my mother's moans and cries through the excruciating long nights of her late stage illness never seeped into my consciousness the next morning at my workplace. This coping mechanism allowed me to participate in life despite the conflicts within my household and within the deep recesses of my mind. The ability to compartmentalize emotions seems to be a positive quality, however my excessiveness caused a complete emotional disconnect that eventually immobilized me because I didn't have the ability to properly experience my emotions. So of course, when the practitioners informed me that I needed intensive treatment for depression during my first hospitalization, I assumed they were harebrained.

I was in denial when I spoke with Diane several months earlier and I remained in denial inside the psychiatric hospital. In my mind, I was exclusively suffering from stress which could be remedied with a few strong tranquilizers. I was unable to connect my feelings of hopelessness, anxiety and defeat to a full blown affliction known as major depression. I felt that I was in control of my decision to give up on my life and, if I so desired, I could reengage with my family, friends and profession at any given time. I blamed myself for my lack of motivation and experienced a deep self loathing. Even though I was unwilling to accept the diagnosis of depression, I did realize that I needed to continue medication therapy for my absurdly self-destructing anxiety once I was released from the hospital.

As a result of being dismissed by Dr. S., I assumed that I was a problematic and unlikeable patient and feared that all psychiatrists would refuse treating me. I was thankful when Dr. K., a Staten Island psychiatrist who I met while I was an inpatient, agreed to treat me at his private practice after my first long-term hospitalization. We made arrangements to have sessions once a week at $100 per session; and I was in treatment with Dr. K. for approximately eight years with a few interruptions. The first few years were financially tolerable because I had savings but eventually my savings were depleted and my astronomical medical and credit card bills caused me to make the difficult decision to file for bankruptcy. It's too bad that Dr. K. and I didn't address my financial burdens because I was emotionally and financially unprepared for the long-term costs of navigating the mental health system. At a certain point I was awarded disability from the government, however, the bankruptcy and Disability Award humiliated me to my very core and reinforced my feelings of low self worth.

"Dr. K., I've decided to decline my Disability Award because there are people who are physically disabled and unable to work and deserve it more than I do."

"Blank, I've been in practice for many years and I could say with certainty that your emotional problems are severely debilitating and you are unable to be gainfully employed. Let's work on balancing your medications and then you can consider going back to work."

Early on Dr. K. tried electroconvulsive therapy or ECT, a procedure whereby electric currents passed through my brain and induced seizures and convulsions that supposedly would rid me of my unhappiness.

"I'm feeling headachy, muddled and detached since you started the treatments, Dr. K."

"Okay, Blank, I'm human after all and I can see that you're much too weak to continue ECT. Your memory will improve in time so don't worry."

Over time, though, I painfully realized that my cognitive abilities and memory loss were permanently impaired and a part of my identity was erased forever.

Dr. K. was a middle-aged Korean gentleman who I respected because he accepted me as a patient even though my case was perceived as challenging. Our language barriers and cultural differences created a discernible division, however the trust that was fostered in our therapeutic relationship was immensely important to me so I ignored some of our barriers. For the most part we discussed the ever-changing adjustments to my drug du jour.

"Dr. K. I feel less anxious, but I'm more depressed."

"Okay, we'll discontinue that drug and start you on MAO Inhibitors and you'll feel better in a few weeks."

After a few weeks passed, I provided Dr. K. with a litany of new side effects:

"Dr. K., now my anxiety is unbearable and I have migraine headaches and my mouth is as dry as a desert."

"Just be patient and give the medications a little more time."

After years of sickening trials of psychotropic drugs, Dr. K. made a confession that was deeply discouraging - but nonetheless true:

"Blank, you're a difficult patient. No matter what drugs we try, your condition remains relatively the same."

Shortly after his confession I observed that Dr. K. gave up on me. Dr. K. knew something back then which I did not – I was never going to recover from depression.

I thought that perhaps Dr. K. was following the wrong treatment plan for my case. He believed that electroconvulsive therapy and antidepressants would balance the chemicals in my brain, but maybe the psychological causes needed to be addressed through intensive talk therapy. I was beginning to wonder if my anxiety and depression had anything at all to do with my brain chemistry.

In hindsight I realize that my psychotropic medications contributed to my depressive illness instead of recovery. Since I existed in a chemically induced state of mind I was unable to fully reengage in those pivotal years of life when an individual starts a family and becomes established in a profession. Eventually I experienced considerable behavioral changes which ultimately distanced the people that were closest to me. Even though Dr. K. offered much-needed consistency in my volatile life, I feel a profound sense of regret that I continued treatment with him at a critical season of my life; however I didn't possess the energy, knowledge, support or confidence to seek alternatives.

My depression and aggressive treatments gave rise to a lifetime of physical pain as well. At times I was taking a cocktail of powerful medications that played havoc on my mind and body. I began to look like a cadaverous version of myself with sunken eyes and a grossly defeated posture. I battled with excessive weight gain and weight loss until I eventually learned to make appropriate dietary changes. The treatments just may have been worse than the depressive disease. In due course I realized that it was time to seek a new treatment method – perhaps I was beginning to feel a sense of hope that things could improve. Even though I stopped believing in my treatment plan, I knew that Dr. K. had the best intentions. Trust opened my heart and connected me to a world that I had forsaken so it was a difficult decision to leave Dr. K., but I finally found the courage to walk away.

My cousin recommended a renowned psychological Institute in Manhattan. It was at one of their workshops that I met David, a psychologist who worked at the Institute. David adhered to the Institute's philosophy which encourages individuals to relinquish their self defeating thoughts and behaviors. I was intrigued by this hopeful rationale and as a result I began treatment with David for the next few years.

At the beginning it was difficult for me to trek from Staten Island to Manhattan for office visits because I had developed a fear of crowded public places and traveling more than a few miles from home triggered anxiety. However, David found ways to help me overcome some of my trepidations by confronting my fears with me. Upon my first session, David accompanied me from Staten Island to his office at the Institute in Manhattan and provided sufficient support and guidance so that I was able to continue this routine independently. After our first session we took a stroll through the city blocks of uptown Manhattan, walking aimlessly by the food vendors and pedestrians that crowded the sidewalks. It had been a long time since I absorbed the aromas, sites, sounds and palpable energy of Manhattan and I was especially grateful to share the experience with someone. That day felt like a celebration of life after being set free from captivity - and in a way I had been held captive for a long time by my own mind.

In a fairly short period of time, my relationship with David evolved into something that would be perceived as inappropriate for a patient and therapist, but I was a consenting adult and years of traditional therapy proved to be unsuccessful and at times downright criminal so I was ready to take a gamble.

The Institute was a townhouse style brick mansion located on the Upper East Side of Manhattan. The interior great hall, lovely hardwood floors and elegant staircase exuded a feeling of old world charm and grandeur. David lived in the basement apartment of the mansion and Dr. E. occupied the penthouse. One evening David introduced me to Dr. E., the founder of a form of therapy which purports that irrational beliefs cause individuals to feel anxious, depressed and angry and lead to self-defeating behaviors. Dr. E. is one of the most influential psychotherapists in history and our brief rendezvous seemed akin to being introduced to Sigmund Freud.

David eventually referred me to Dr. B., a prominent physician, best-selling author and host of his own radio talk show. His extraordinary education and practice of using holistic medicine and treating the brain, body and spirit as a whole presented further hope for treatment of my depression. My initial visit consisted of hours of physical and psychological testing, including a brain scan known as the BEAM brain test. I met Dr. B. after the battery of tests were completed and was immediately drawn to his handsome appearance and charismatic demeanor.

"Blank, your brain scan demonstrates something slightly peculiar. We should look into this a little further at some point. Otherwise you appear to be physically healthy. I would like to start you on psychotropic medications immediately. After reviewing your tests and speaking with you for a while, I find your depression and anxiety to be severe and I'm concerned that you are not being honest with me about your suicidal ideation. In fact, I'm not certain that you'll follow through with taking your medications so I'd like you to come to the office weekly and my Physician's Assistant will administer antidepressants by injections."

"Dr. B., I came to you for an alternative treatment. I was thinking that maybe you would find hormonal imbalances and then offer a diet and supplementation program that would ease my symptoms."

"Blank, of course proper nutrition and supplements will benefit you, but I think you need immediate help so I recommend starting the injections today."

His Physician's Assistant escorted me directly into an exam room and jabbed my thigh with a large needle. The injections must have been absorbed into my muscles fairly quickly because I recall the pain and stiffness in my legs as I dishearteningly made the long trip back home. It was my hope that Dr. B. would eventually see an improvement and then consider another treatment, but that never happened. A short time after receiving the injection I began to suffer an unbearable reaction to the medication.   I called Dr. B. for help and tried to explain my familiar but ambiguous symptoms.

"Dr. B. I don't know what's wrong with me. In the past doctors told me these symptoms were all in my mind, but my instincts are telling me that it has something to do with the medications."

"Blank, come back to my office. I think I know what's wrong."

I don't know how I managed to make it to his office because the symptoms were torturous and I felt like jumping off the Gowanus Expressway while on my way back to New York City. But the thing that surely keeps me in balance is the knowledge that I have support and I knew Dr. B. was going to do his best to help.

"Hi Blank, please have a seat and tell me more about what's going on with you."

I have always been able to exercise some degree of control over my mind and body while under duress and standing before someone, but this was beyond my control and I was embarrassed by my involuntary behavior, although I think I put up a good front.

"It's so terribly strange, but I can't sit for more than a few seconds because every nerve in my body is being attacked by something indescribable. It's a feeling so overwhelming that it is affecting both my mind and body. I'm compelled to remain in motion every waking hour for the last few days. As soon as I sit I need to stand and vise versa."

"Blank, you're suffering from a condition known as akathesia. It's a rare reaction from the antidepressants. I'm going to give you antihistamines and we'll discontinue the current antidepressant and start you on a new one once you're feeling better."

I was deeply discouraged and decided not to see Dr. B. again. After years of unbearable side effects, I didn't have the strength to endure another round. However, after a decade of misdiagnosis and inappropriate remedies which only served to exasperate the symptoms of akathesia, I was grateful and relieved when Dr. B. defined the syndrome upon a brief observation of my condition. Dr. B. validated the unnecessary hell that I experienced through the years and the ignorance of the psychiatrists that treated me before him. It was at this very moment that I completely ceased trusting all psychiatrists.

I never underwent further tests to discover why my brain scan was not normal. I've always wondered if further exploration of my brain could help doctors discover a reliable treatment plan for my depression. Perhaps one day I'll have the strength, support and courage to go back to Dr. B. for answers although I realize that at times knowledge is power and at other times ignorance is bliss. If I never have the opportunity to visit Dr. B. again, my plan is to donate my abnormal brain to science in hopes that neuroscientists could discover the underlying causes of sad emotions – and ultimately a cure for depression. I wonder if that's considered grandiose thinking.

I continued to see David but our relationship was challenged shortly after he was displaced from his basement apartment at the Institute. After 20 years of service to the Institute, Dr. E. asked him to leave the premises at once because of differences of opinion however David never explained the disagreement in detail.

David temporarily moved in with a married couple who were both psychologists that lived near the Institute. I visited David at their apartment on a number of occasions and was dismayed after witnessing a volatile situation in which three psychologists were unable to resolve their personal conflicts peacefully and effectively. I always looked up to psychologists and psychiatrists to be the voice of reason and experts on human behavior, but I learned through my years in therapy that they are just regular folks with human foibles and oftentimes they are disappointedly unreasonable.

David eventually became displaced again and moved in with me and my father for several months. He was having financial difficulties because he lost most of his patients, his teaching position at one of the New York City universities and his gig as a ski instructor. David was the epitome of an absent minded professor, a talented academic who focused almost exclusively on studying holistic medicine while forgetting to concentrate on things like relationship and career development. Without clear boundaries in our shared intimate space our relationship became so confusing that David decided to wear a cap when he was assuming the role of my therapist and he removed the cap when he was assuming the role of my friend. Unfortunately the cap method did not resolve our problems and our relationship eventually dissolved. David's last words to me not only hurt my feelings but physically hurt, as if he were throwing stones at my heart.

"Blank, I don't consider you a friend and it's my professional opinion that you have too many problems to be able to sustain a friendship with anyone."

Sadly, that statement rang true. Even though our relationship was confusing and challenging, I cared about David and I certainly SHOULD have been a better friend. But as David would tell me if he were here:

"Blank, never 'SHOULD' on yourself!"

With time and distance I can objectively say that David's wounding words helped me to make positive changes in my relationships. The ambiguous roles of therapist and friend were just a hiccup in our relationship; the larger problems existed long before I met David. David's progressive therapeutic methods and his willingness to defy conventional therapy was undeniably healing, however when he moved in with me I felt a loss of control in maintaining boundaries and resorted to expressing myself through anger. Anger is one of the tactics that I subconsciously use when I'm trying to protect myself from the possibility of being hurt and avoidance is the other. Since then I learned to keep my relationship weaknesses in check and whenever I realize that I'm responsible for bringing negativity into a relationship I remind myself of the importance of offering friends the love, patience, acceptance and respect that they deserve.

I am grateful for many of the life lessons that I learned from David, like discovering that I could feel symptom improvement with the generous support of a caring person. Love and companionship are the elixirs for my depression. Another life lesson he taught me, and I know you can benefit as well, is to practice until it becomes habit, replacing self-defeating thoughts with self-affirming thoughts. So on the subject of perfectionism, for example, I now attempt to replace thoughts like: 'If I inadvertently offend someone I'm a bad person' with thoughts like: 'I will try not to offend anyone, but it's human to make mistakes some of the time.' It's difficult to always be cognizant of my self-defeating thoughts, but I do try because I know the importance of developing a more positive perspective and accepting the human aspects of the self.

Nevertheless, gratitude and a few life lessons did not bring about peace of mind. I was still severely anxious, depressed and the loss of my friendship with David reinforced my issues of low self esteem and guilt. Dr. K. and I treated my symptoms chemically while David and I treated my symptoms rationally and unfortunately both therapies were unsuccessful. I didn't know very much about the clinical styles available in psychology, but speculated that I needed a therapist who would help me visit the demons existing deep within my subconscious.

Feeling dismayed, I wondered whether the financial and emotional toll of therapy was worth it. I needed the human connection but the process of finding a good therapist seemed unachievable since I didn't know anyone who could offer reliable recommendations. In addition, I was acutely aware that I was not an ideal patient. What therapist would want me as a patient with my treatment resistant depression, my negative tone and tenor during therapeutic conversations, my abandonment issues and my annoying tardiness?

I tried to be without the support from a therapist for a while, but almost immediately missed the sanctuary of a therapist's office where I could safely relax on a couch and share my narrative with a receptive listener. I was still unable to establish friendships because I could not free myself from the gravitational pull of my depression, so once again I began to withdraw from human connection and the world. I only left the house to visit my mother at the nursing home which day after day reeked of despair. When my suppressed thoughts and feelings became lodged deep in my chest and the grip of loneliness and isolation had become unbearable, I decided to seek help from a therapist once again.

I noticed Dr. D.s office conveniently located between my home and the nursing home so I timidly contacted him. He agreed to see me as his patient in 2001 shortly before my mother passed away and we parted directly after my father passed away five years later. Today the entirety of my relationship with Dr. D. reminds me of parental death.

Dr. D. was an older gentleman who had a weekly advice column in the local newspaper and seemed to be a pillar of the community. I felt protected in Dr. D's small basement office, as if I were safely hidden under the surface of reality. Dr. D. rarely provided self-disclosure, but this seemed preferable to my open relationship with David at first. Unfortunately, it was impossible for me to form an authentic therapeutic relationship with him because of his anonymity and because I began to see him as a father figure. I never experienced the depth of these baffling feelings in any other relationship and until today my emotions have only been addressed in the writing of this book.

My inappropriate redirection of feelings from my actual father onto my therapist is known in therapy as transference. The concept of transference was established by Sigmund Freud when he observed that many of his patients were falling in love with him and he realized that their feelings could not have been brought about by his personal attributes. This phenomenon is not just limited to therapy, although an individual is especially susceptible to transference in therapy. The common result of transference is that we don't treat others as they truly are but who we subconsciously want them to be. At times transference could have a positive outcome because it gives a therapist power to help a patient with past wounds, however, in my case it was almost deadly.

Dr. D. eventually began to reveal himself during a period when I was experiencing a series of especially difficult episodes which included the ending of my relationship with a boyfriend on New Year's Eve in 2005. It had been years since I had been involved in a personal relationship with a man, except for my unconventional relationship with David. I decided to accept a dinner invitation from a grief stricken co-worker weeks after the tragic loss of his young son and we began dating shortly thereafter. I was particularly vulnerable at this time because it had been in the early years of my reentrance into the workforce and into the world. He portrayed himself as a man of means and from the beginning professed that he wanted to provide the children and family that I so deeply desired. However, when it came close to the time we were to live with one another, he told me that he only had a few months to live and wanted to spend his remaining days alone. My anxiety about his well-being and my feelings of loss were insufferable.

Several weeks later a mutual acquaintance informed me that he was openly dating someone else. The sudden and striking realization that his terminal illness was a fabrication and our relationship was a sham caused me to spiral into another deep depression. I can't imagine how someone could be so heartless as to lie about their impending death and I speculate that this man fits the profile of a sociopath because of his outlandish lies, superficial charm and authoritarian manner, among other things. I am responsible for my choices, but the truth was deeply hidden somewhere in my empathy over the loss of a man's son, a cancer diagnosis, and promises of a fulfilling future and I was seeing things through a tangled web of lies and confusion.

"Dr. D., I should have known it wasn't possible for a man to care about me."

"Blank, sometimes a person of his character preys on the weaknesses and needs of others. It struck me for a while that he was unkind to you and dishonest."

"Why didn't you tell me your feelings before?"

Dr. D. went back into a role of the silent analyst, but when I looked directly into his eyes I saw a tear running down his cheek. I found his unspoken empathy to be among my most healing moments in therapy.

Dr. D. also revealed himself when my father was diagnosed with late stage cancer the following year. I was unable to see Dr. D. on a regular basis during this period but he began to call me routinely and we had reassuring, genuine conversations. I always imagined that Dr. D. only existed one hour a week in his basement office and after our session he magically disappeared. But sure enough Dr. D. was calling me from home and though we were separated by bridges and boroughs he very much existed beyond the therapeutic door. Dr. D. became real to me, but I now wonder if I was real to him.

Although I saw Dr. D. as a father image, I was about to find out that he was nothing like my father because my father never abandoned the people closest to him despite my mother's illness. My parents had the benevolent ability to treat everyone they met as their family – how wonderful the world would be if everyone felt this way. I'm remorseful for believing that Dr. D. could ever replace my father in any way and my energy would have been best spent trying to develop a closer relationship with my real father.

It's humiliating to divulge, but the perilous result of creating an idealized paternal transference was that I had expectations that Dr. D. would help pull me from the wreckage of my loss and guide me through an uncertain future, as a father would. In the past he was able to incorporate a sense of authority into my life, supporting me through difficult times, and I assumed that he would remain committed to my well-being when I went to see him almost directly after my father's funeral.

"Dr. D., I feel intense guilt over my relationship with my father as an adult. I had become so distant with him and I abandoned him in the end."

"Blank, you're a good and giving person. You just fought the entire healthcare system so that your father could receive better care. What more could you have done?"

"I was with my father in the doctor's office the day that he was diagnosed with lung cancer. Upon the diagnosis I abruptly walked out of the office for a little while so that I could take care of my own emotional needs. Several weeks later, when my father was in the New York City hospital, I asked him why he didn't wait for me when difficult test results were being presented to him - and his response still keeps me awake at night."

"What did your father say that's so disturbing?"

"He candidly let me know that it wasn't necessary to seek my support since I couldn't handle the day in the doctor's office when he was diagnosed. I really let him down in so many ways and over the course of so many years. Why does death have to be so final? Maybe if I had children I could right some of the wrongs of my relationship with my own parents or at the very least I could be distracted from the pain and guilt surrounding their life and death."

Shortly after that session Dr. D. called me to cancel our next appointment.

"Blank, my wife is not feeling well. I need to cancel this Tuesday. I'll call you in a few days to reschedule an appointment for next week."

I waited for Dr. D. to call to reschedule our weekly sessions but I did not hear from him. I understood that Dr. D.'s wife needed him but I couldn't understand why he did not follow-up with another telephone call. The fact was that I needed my therapist and I speculated that many of his patients were in the same distress. I recalled a conversation that I had with Dr. D. one evening on the subject of abandonment.

"Sometimes I worry that you'll suddenly disappear from my life. I've come to depend on you over the years."

"Just keep in mind that we've known one another for a long time and I'm always here for our weekly sessions. That's enough precedent to show you that I'm not going to abandon you."

With this conversation in mind, I assumed something must be terribly wrong or Dr. D. would have reached out to me. I eventually called Dr. D., but he did not return my call. I continued to leave messages through the weeks, each message a little more frantic than the last, but still he did not return my calls. There were days when I imagined that he was gravely ill and was physically unable to call me and there were days when I speculated that he simply discarded me as if I were rubbish. It was difficult to accept that he would leave his practice without providing reasonable notice or assistance in my transition to see another therapist so that my care was not interrupted.

The sudden separation from my father and my idealized father created a deep sense of longing and when we are longing for something our hearts perpetually explore ways to be reunited. I feverishly attempted to find answers so that my heart could be free from anxious discontent.

Finally I met Dr. D.'s colleague who had the answer to my emotionally weighted question.

"I'm a patient of Dr. D.'s and it appears that he has abandoned his practice. I'm wondering if you could tell me if he's okay."

"Yes, I've seen him recently and he seems to be fine."

His response brought conclusions to my mind that slashed at my heart leaving wounds that are still gushing. If Dr. D. was okay then I was a victim of neglectful abandonment and he violated the very foundation of our therapeutic alliance. Dr. D. was irretrievably lost to me and I needed to come to terms with the fact that it wasn't in his heart to terminate our therapeutic relationship with compassion. Furthermore, there are clear ethical guidelines which maintain that a therapist should never abandon or neglect a patient. It is required that therapists coordinate satisfactory arrangements so that treatment is continued during periods of interruptions or termination. Anything less, especially with a patient who may be in crisis, is unconscionable.

Yet - I quickly came to the conclusion that I deserved the betrayal because I was also the perpetrator of the unconscionable abandonment of my father when he received his cancer diagnosis and I left the room. Perhaps it was perfect karma at work and this was the emotional debt that I needed to pay. The simultaneous loss of my father and a father image irrecoverably cemented my lifelong fears of abandonment and depression. I never experienced this degree of anguish in my life.

As a result of Dr. D.'s actions I've learned valuable lessons on abandonment. I now make arduous attempts not to abandon anyone or anything that is important to me. I'm still working on overcoming my fears of abandonment by continuously reminding myself to separate my past from the present. I believe that healing from abandonment issues can only be possible if I learn to trust, however it's difficult for me to trust anyone because I have been abandoned so many times and in so many ways. Sometimes abandonment issues can be resolved in therapy, but ironically I need to first trust my relationship with a therapist before I can heal.

So I began my grieving process without support from a therapist. My mother's death was cataclysmic because it forced me to acknowledge mortality and the fragility of life for the first time; and my father's death filled my heart with an unearthly hopelessness because I was acutely aware of my aloneness and knew that the void would never be filled. Since the very evening of my father's passing, I return to an empty home each night where there is a palpable emptiness that can't be described. Everything that my parents represented in terms of love, security, and family were gone. I remember expressing these feelings to my brother back then and his heartfelt response was healing:

"Blank, we may not have a close relationship at this time, but we can try to begin a new and different kind of relationship now that dad's gone."

My brother's sentiments were poignant and I looked forward to building a relationship with him, but he had a family of his own with obligations and as the months progressed I was still incredibly lonely despite his kind support. I decided it was in my best interest to seek professional help once again. I was hoping to find a therapist who had the ability to understand and empathize with my fears and anguish and help me discover a sense of direction now that I no longer had a meaningful role in my life. Frankly, I was hoping to find a therapist who could help me find a reason to live.

Finding a therapist was becoming more problematic through the years because there is a significant shortage of available, mature and skilled psychologists that are part of the health insurance plan networks in Staten Island. In addition, I was seen as a difficult patient because of the severity of my depression and several therapists refused to take my case. Although I can easily define the ways in which I'm difficult, I never knew for certain what their individual rationale was behind my label.

Eventually an acquaintance recommended my current therapist, Blank2, whom she knew through her business. I immediately attempted to contact his office and left a voice message but my call was never returned. Soon after, my acquaintance personally called Blank2 on my behalf and he agreed to see me as a favor to her.

While driving to my first appointment I became preoccupied with racing thoughts and found myself totally lost and wandering around the south shore of Staten Island, eventually barreling into Blank2's office embarrassed about my tardiness. Not only was I embarrassed but I felt shame knowing I was a difficult patient and that Blank2 only agreed to a first meeting because of our mutual acquaintance.

Through the eyes of anxiety I began to see the office décor with increasing clarity. It was comfortable and ordinary, a filing cabinet, coffee table, chair, desk and a shabby couch. What struck me the most was the intermittent rumbling sounds of nearby trains passing through, but essentially the mood of the environment was calming. As the session progressed I was consoled by Blank2's amiable disposition and began to feel somewhat at ease in his presence. I told him a little about my personal history and he shared a little about his life.

"I'm a professor at a local university and I'm happily married with two children. My father recently passed away so I understand your grief."

My momentary feeling of connection vanished in an instant when I compared the emotional distance of our grief. Blank2 could not see how physically and emotionally alone I was and I wondered if I could form a relationship with someone who didn't understand my default language of isolation. I was uncharacteristically straight forward about my feelings considering we had just met.

"There is a difference in our grief. Since my father's death I've been literally alone almost all of the time and what's more painful is the knowledge that if and when the initial shock and despondency of my father's loss is diminished - I will continue to be alone."

"Blank, often when a person is grieving they feel alone, even people like me with a family of my own."

Blank2 was right to defend his grief. No one should ever compare the emotional intensity of grief because we could never fully understand the heartache of another. Comparing grief deprives a person of their worth and I immediately felt guilty. The truth is that I liked Blank2 upon our first meeting and wanted to express my sympathy, but I built too many walls around me and needed to protect myself. I was comforted by the fact that our childhood socioeconomic backgrounds appeared to be similar and we were of the same age because I assumed these parallels would become a good foundation for an effective therapeutic alliance.

Before the session ended I presented my most difficult emotional issues so that Blank2 could determine whether he wanted to continue treatment with me and if not there would be nothing lost and nothing gained. I was thankful when Blank2 agreed to work with me and in July 2006 a new therapeutic relationship was born with a therapist and patient in the midst of mourning the loss of their fathers.

As much as I liked Blank2, I was unable to form a close therapeutic bond with him over my first few years in treatment. He was friendly but in an emotionally detached and noncommittal sort of way and despite my fears of abandonment I really needed to feel a bond with a therapist. I tried to analyze the reason for the roadblock and speculated that perhaps Blank2 was simply disinterested in me. I also wondered if I had become too damaged to trust again. I began to cancel sessions which is unlike me because I'm obsessive about following through on all my appointments, especially as it relates to therapy.

Yet for some indefinable reason I believed that it was important for me to continue seeing Blank2 at that juncture in my life; and I'm thankful that I endured because the course of my therapy was profoundly transformed when Blank2 requested something from me during one of our sessions.

"Blank, I have a favor to ask you. My best buddy and I designed a website where people could share their thoughts and feelings on the subject of hope. I'd like you to consider writing your thoughts on hope for my new website."

"But, I'm not a good writer and I'm one of the most hopeless individuals that you'll ever meet."

"I'm very excited about the website and would really appreciate if you just made an effort to write anything that comes to mind."

"Okay, I'll try."

Blank2 never asked a favor of me so he certainly deserved my consideration. I went home that evening and dwelled upon the abstruse concept of hope. Through the late hours of the night images of hope were haunted by unsettling images of hopelessness. The concept of hope, I found, cannot be understood unless I considered its opposite. We can't fully appreciate the glory of rising up to the heavens unless we understand what it is like to descend into hell's inferno. After a long night I formulated a few small paragraphs that incorporated my feelings of hope and haltingly handed my assignment to Blank2 upon the end of our next session. I swiftly left his office because I was too insecure to stick around for his critique. In my wildest imagination I never anticipated his feedback when we met again the following week.

"I was able to connect with your concept of hope and so did my wife and best buddy. We are going to add an editorial link and we would like you to be a regular contributor. I would like you to consider writing some more on the subject of hope."

The ability to connect with Blank2 and others through writing was an awesome experience. For the first time in my life I felt a little less alone and consequently was inspired to write again. Perhaps, I thought, I could help other lonely people find a voice and connection as well. So as time went on I found ways to write about hope despite my limited writing skills. As a person with a chaotic personal history, I wanted to discover ways in which people could find hope in the midst of sheer devastation and began to consider subjects like the September 11th terrorist attacks, the 2010 oil spill in the Gulf of Mexico and the devastating tsunami in Japan in 2011.

I've come to feel a sense of healing as a result of my connection with Blank2 through writing, however the ebb and flow of energy in a therapeutic alliance, like any relationship, brings difficult challenges. At times I become defensive or detached because of my fears of abandonment, especially since our relationship is presumed to be finite. As a result of my fears, sustained tension and disconnection permeate the therapy room throughout the session and every so often the negative emotions persist for as long as several months. During those periods I feel as if I'm stuck in a turbulent holding pattern on an aircraft and I do not know if I will ever land safely.

Sometimes there are practical problems in the therapeutic relationship. In the early fall of 2015, Blank2 and I struggled with a barrier that was imposed by my health insurance carrier when they abruptly terminated my coverage for therapy.

"Blank, I need to inform you that your insurance carrier has stopped paying for your visits with me. It's my opinion that you need therapy so I'm going to submit an appeal and for now I'll accept your co-payments as full compensation for your sessions."

"If their decision is not in our favor I don't think I can continue to see you. I feel like I'm being abandoned at the end of a road. Why are they doing this to me?"

"They don't believe that you're showing progress. What are your thoughts?"

"It's clear to me that the insurance company is discriminating against people who live with chronic mental illnesses that may need treatment over a lifetime. They would never deny payments for chronic physical conditions, like diabetes. A cardiologist wouldn't be in a position to tell his patient that the insurance company will stop covering medical expenses if their congenital heart disease doesn't show improvement."

"Blank, I absolutely agree."

Sadly our battle with the insurance company affects many people who are in need of behavioral health services. Insurance companies are erroneously given the right to determine if therapy is medically necessary even though it's in their best interest to find loopholes to support not paying claims.

The Affordable Care Act has been transforming the way health care is provided since 2010. The Mental Health.gov website states the following: "The Affordable Care Act provides one of the largest expansions of mental health and substance use disorder coverage in a generation, by requiring that most individual and small employer health insurance plans...cover mental health and substance use disorder services... These new protections build on the Mental Health Parity and Addiction Equity Act of 2008 provisions to expand mental health and substance use disorder benefits and federal parity protections to an estimated 62 million Americans."

I am thankful for these changes; however mental health benefits continue to face critical obstacles and discrimination that need immediate attention. One of the problems is that psychologists are battling with insurance companies whenever they treat patients with chronic mental illnesses, like a severe depressive disorder. The insurance carriers require that psychologists document progress; however progress for individuals with chronic depressive disorders is not always possible or the progress may be imperceptible and therefore cannot be measured by conventional standards - but this does not negate the effectiveness of therapy.

For those with chronic mental illnesses, success is sometimes measured by the ability to maintain balance. As a case in point, I live with nightmarish feelings of instability every waking moment and a mere fender bender or a sly remark can cause me to tumble down on my knees in excruciating emotional pain. The regularity of psychotherapy helps me to find enough emotional balance to dust off my knees and face the world once again.

When patients are denied access to the right care they will not be able to maintain the best possible quality of life and it's the chronic cases that are most often denied the help that they need. Sometimes the life of a person with mental illness can begin to fall apart when treatment is only briefly interrupted. Some may take their own lives because they are unable to handle their chronic suffering alone; some with psychotic symptoms may cause harm to society as we witness in recurring media coverage. When we realize that these seriously ill people in the media sought treatment, but their health insurance providers refused to cover them for long-term care, it seems unconscionable – yet insurance companies are still given the right to make these decisions. When will our government wake up to the disproportionate allocation of resources of mental health services?

Not long ago Blank2 presented a vital query when we were considering the effectiveness of psychotherapy:

"Blank, do you think therapy helps you?"

"I know that I continue to feel depressed and I still have a difficult time coping with everyday problems. But while I might not show progress on paper, I'm certain that my symptoms would spiral without the help of a therapist."

Since then I have given Blank2's query further consideration and I have come to realize that all of my therapists helped me to endure at one time or another. Every relationship affects us in both negative and positive ways and with the benefit of time I am able to appreciate the unquestionable positive aspects of my therapeutic relationships through the years. My chronic depression left me utterly broken and Dr. K., David, and Dr. D. helped me to pick up the pieces of my shattered life and one by one they gave me a reason to live. I was able to form a powerful human bond with my therapists and I still mourn their loss just as I mourn the loss of anyone significant in my life that has moved on or passed away.

My longest therapeutic relationship has been with my current therapist, Blank2. Even though I do not show progress he has not given up on me and that in itself gives me hope. Blank2 has helped me break through some of the silent pain of depression with psychotherapy and through the journey of writing. And, with Blank2's continued support it is my hope that I will be able to make positive changes in my life and find acceptance for the things that I cannot change.

Despite my losses and setbacks in therapy, I maintain profound gratitude for a discipline that has the power to diminish the misery of depression and loneliness - and for now - that's my final analysis.

Reflections on Chapter 15: Therapy

I recall being passionately immersed in the writing of this chapter some years ago. My goals were to reveal the difficulties I experienced in therapy with accurate details so that the reader would understand the true depth of emotions in long-term therapy; and the reasons I still value the discipline despite its complexity. This is the only chapter in my book where I have an intuitive sense that I accomplished what I set out to do.

As I look back on decades of therapy I am horrified by some of my mistakes, nonetheless, therapy is the road I have travelled and these are some of the valuable lessons I have learned:

Firstly, it is important to find a therapist who is compassionate, committed, insightful, academically and emotionally intelligent, and is determined to never give up despite the nature of chronic depression. We may not be in control of the behavior of therapists, but we are in control of our own choices.

Secondly, once a good therapeutic alliance is formed I am certain that therapy is an effective treatment for depression as I have personally witnessed its curative effect. Therapy is indispensible for those who suffer from afflictions of the mind.

Chapter Sixteen

DAWN TO DARK

At 6:00 a.m. the sun glimmers through my bedroom window slowly casting shades of light on broken dreams and I awake, like a blank page, void of emotional content, waiting for my story to be written. In the still and silent morning air I regress to a sweet time in my life when I was young and at the threshold of a promising open door. I am perpetually stuck in that watershed moment at the Golden Gate Bridge decades ago when my major depressive disorder brought my life to a jarring halt. As the growing dawn arouses my reality I try to fantasize about going back in time to mend all the broken pieces that shaped the trajectory of my life, but I come to realize that my past has been written in stone - so I grieve my losses once again.

Eyes fully open, no longer in a daze, I resign myself to the pulse and energy of a new day and I try to muster up enough courage and strength to surrender my refuge. There is an especially palpable feeling of isolation at the beginning and ending of each day, knowing that at these pivotal times I am completely alone – no one to care for and no one to care for me. For many years I craved independence, never realizing it would come at a price. I thought that living alone would improve the quality of my life, a possible liberation from my inner demons. I yearned for solitude when I didn't fully understand the pain of abiding loneliness. Now I sadly reminisce about the clamorous mornings of days gone by.

"Dad, must you make espresso coffee at 6:00 a.m. in the morning? The strong aroma wakes me up. Could you please try to keep the noise at a minimum?"

"Blank, I live here and I'm going to make a little noise from time to time. Would you prefer to wake up alone without any family at all?"

I certainly asked too much of my father back then. Damn all my sensitivities and damn me for making my father's mornings so difficult.

The internal dialogue rattles through my brain as I make an effort to rise from the comfort of my bed. My feet finally reach the cold, hard floor and I shuffle through my apartment wondering whether the loss of balance and weakness is a result of my sleeping medications or my depression. Research shows that the morning is especially difficult for depressives because of changes in hormones, among many other things. As a result, many depressives share similar symptoms in the morning, like feeling depleted of energy, difficulty getting out of bed, increased agitation and sadness. Knowledge about symptoms does not equal healing, so I endure and strive to have a productive day even though it seems so out of reach at the first blush of morning.

I follow a regimented morning routine which helps to relieve some of my anxiety. I open shades, shower, care for my dog, and prepare my usual breakfast of oatmeal hoping that a warm meal will nourish the emptiness that consumes me. While eating breakfast my anxiety churns my insides as I think about my responsibilities at work, paying bills, home maintenance issues and the likelihood that there is a full stressful day ahead of me. I'm already wound up and my limited physical and emotional resources are exhausted, so I take the time to practice my secret meditative ritual so that I could find a semblance of balance.

I begin by inserting ear plugs in my ears to protect me from noise because the anxiety I experience as a result of my noise sensitivity will make it impossible to mediate. Then I turn on soft music, sit on my sofa and engage in a meditative mind game. The purpose of my creative game is to divert my attention from negative stimuli and ultimately find my way back to a peaceful balance. I start by recalling clear and vivid descriptions of simple joys, such as some of the objects I appreciate in my apartment. Then I close my eyes and mentally describe the glossy white porcelain floor tiles in diamond-shaped patterns, the black cast iron miniature chandelier with crystal drops, and the various shades of taupe paint on my living room and dining room walls, etc. As I become relaxed my mind automatically begins to wander however at that point in the meditative process I am no longer in control of where my thoughts take me. If I am successful in incorporating some distance between my consciousness and stressful stimuli my mind begins to become numb and my trembling breath becomes steady and calm. This process is like a natural anesthetic however it is an uneasy calm that could be shattered with the sound of an ant walking across the room.

Mind wandering and meditative behaviors are actually a natural state of our brain at rest and we all engage in these practices, consciously or subconsciously. However for me it is an excessive habit and it's the uncontrollable excessive nature of things that are known as a psychological disorder. If I were forced to feel raw emotional pain without periods of rest I would probably go completely mad. Whenever I resist this ritual my depressive and anxiety symptoms intensify and it becomes almost impossible to conceal my insidious depressive illness to the outside world.

I am like the classic tale of Brer Rabbit and the Tar-Baby. The Tar-Baby is a doll made of sticky tar that is used to trap Brer Rabbit. The more Brer Rabbit attempts to fight with the Tar-Baby the more he becomes trapped. Similarly, when I attempt to resist my numbing process I become more and more trapped into a stressful state of mind and begin to make personal and professional errors that are beyond repair. I have heard it said that what we most resist – persists.

I never explored the subject of meditation so I'm unable to discern the difference between traditional meditation and my innate meditative practice. I can only say that traditional meditation reduces stress and promotes positive moods while my meditative practice is maladaptive and ultimately contributes to my depression. I squander too much precious time absorbed in this meditative process and I often imagine how different my life would be if I were able to utilize those hours fulfilling goals and giving something of myself to humanity. Nonetheless this is my reality and I must persevere. Today is about survival, but I will keep hope in my heart that things will improve.

At 8:00 a.m. I clean up the dishes and finish dressing for work. If I have a little extra time in the morning I work on my book. My anxiety is subdued but my depression remains severe; perhaps my mind subconsciously drifted to where my sad heart had taken it. Carrying out the mundane tasks of preparing for work is taxing because my depression has caused a weakness which slows down my physical movements. I yearn for feelings of well-being so that I could swiftly get through my routines. Once there was a time when my motivation to be productive outweighed my fatigue and I was capable of starting my day at the break of dawn. Today my very being demands that I remain frozen in time, anesthetized and defeated, because my depression has won its battle in the game of life.

At approximately 10:00 a.m. I am almost ready to head to work. I only take positions where I can start in the later hours of the morning because of my unmanageable depressive symptoms. I double-check that all electrical appliances are shut off, my dog is safe and comfortable and the door is locked. As I take the elevator downstairs I'm unable to feel a sense of ease so I go back to my apartment and check everything once again. If I don't recheck everything I will be unable to shake the feeling that I will cause irreparable damage to myself or someone else. Intellectually I understand that this is irrational thinking but nonetheless I am compelled to carry out this routine every time I leave my apartment. My checking rituals are time consuming and as a result I'm often late for work or an appointment. For instance, when I check if I locked my front door properly I don't simply turn the doorknob – I check if there is a malfunction in the entire lock mechanism, if the bolt and door are lined up properly and if I turned my keys in the proper direction. I check the lock over and over again until I feel confident enough that my dog and apartment are secure.

As I drive to my office my anxiety begins to peak because soon I will need to modify my behavior, like a chameleon, so that I will be accepted in my office environment. I continue to work part-time hours because whenever I increase my hours my depression and anxiety become intensified and maintaining a precarious balance in every aspect of my life helps to control my symptoms. I still do not disclose information about my disability to my employers unless I need to request a reasonable adjustment of my responsibilities or my work schedule. Actually, I do not tell most people about depression because it's so widely misunderstood. I cringe whenever I see the ubiquitous television advertisements for Abilify and other antidepressants which portray depression using lighthearted cartoon characters to represent an insufferable disease. Advertising has a significant effect on perception and it is important for the public to understand the gravity of severe and untreatable depression.

Despite my depression, I attempt to be pleasant with my co-workers because each of us is responsible for the energy we emit to the people in our environment. I've come to enjoy some of the positive social interactions at work - but still I am often on the outside of most social interactions. I have a reputation of being compliant and possessing good work ethics - but most of my required tasks, especially new tasks, create crippling anxiety. When things go well at the office, both socially and professionally, I feel so wonderfully blessed and humbled that I almost forget about all of my limitations.

Unemployment among those that suffer from chronic depression is high especially in the current economy so I persistently confront my challenges – and hope for another good day.

After work I handle personal errands. I prefer going grocery shopping and to establishments that provide services in the evening because they are generally less crowded and therefore less stressful for me. These days I've been experiencing difficulty with my depression when I'm in department stores, supermarkets or any type of large box stores. I tried to explain my quandary to Blank2.

"Whenever I walk into a large store lately I feel incredibly sad and I need to run out as soon as possible. It's been harder than usual getting my errands done."

"Can you describe the feeling?"

I feel frustrated whenever Blank2 asks me to describe a feeling because it's always difficult for me to quickly process my emotions. Regardless, I attempt to describe my feelings because increasing awareness and self observation is important in therapy.

"Maybe I'm coining a new phrase but when I enter a crowded store it feels as if I'm experiencing - *a depression attack.* Instead of the sudden onset of fear and apprehension of anxiety attacks, I'm feeling a sudden onset of hopelessness and despair and I need to quickly exit the store in order to suppress the pain."

"Blank, do you know why this is happening?"

"I have no idea."

"Maybe it's because you're feeling alone in a crowd."

I didn't mention this to Blank2 but I believe his theory has some validity.

It is approximately 7:00 p.m. and I finally turn the key to a door that opens to the piercing sound of emptiness. I call out to my sweet dog and wearily surrender to the solitude of my home. I tend to my dog and change into something more comfortable. Then I prepare dinner, usually fast foods since cooking for one is too laborious and offers little reward. I eat standing over the kitchen counter or sitting on the sofa because eating at the table evokes feelings of loneliness and profound cravings for companionship. The loneliness of the day fills me with an oppressive sense of foreboding in the evening.

In the solitude of my home I am liberated from the pressures of what society expects of me and I begin to examine my day. And once examined I feel the guilt, regret and shame over the moments when I may have offended someone and the numerous mistakes that were made during the day. In the solitude of my home I feel the hurts of humanity and each man's hurts become a part of me - and I am diminished.

My depression is insufferable in the witching hours of night because I am physically and emotionally drained; and if anything occurs beyond routine, like an unexpected bill or a plumbing problem, I am immobilized. When I am under duress my world is unfixable and my emotions are unpredictable. Even the sound of doors slamming in the common area of my apartment building seems akin to physical torture and intensifies my all-consuming negative emotions.

I am like an emotional volcano and all of the heated anxieties and sadness of my day need to spew just like hot lava and ashes need to burst from the earth's surface. The more I try to suppress my fiery emotions the more the pressure builds up. I stay in constant movement in hopes that the powerful energy will dissipate with physical exertion, but the putrid soot and ashes raging within me have no escape so they painfully linger. With no one to call or turn to I literally sink to the cold, dank ground in despair. I try to cry, but it is a suffocated cry, only capable of resonating within my heart and soul. There is no escape, no release. Gradually my racing thoughts are anesthetized by hopelessness and the world fades away for a little while.

Once I am drawn back to reality I feel detached from my body and emotions as if I have vacated my body and I am watching it from above. My detached self observes a forlorn middle aged woman with a posture that has grown weary. The fiery emotions boiling within me have been quelled – but not set free.

Unfortunately these merciless moments are frequent and unyielding in tenacity. If it is a reasonable hour and I'm feeling especially hopeless I call Blank2 for help.

"It's Blank and I'm not feeling well."

"Are you feeling better now?"

"Yes. Maybe I could use an extra session this week."

Blank2 never really knows how to respond to my vague statements but over the years he has become accustomed to my peculiar cry for help. We usually speak for just a few minutes but ultimately the length of our conversation is unimportant as long as I come away feeling a sense of connection with someone who cares.

As the grey early evening changes into black night, I find myself incapable of doing anything even remotely challenging because I have drained my physical and emotional resources and I'm functioning on empty. I wind down by doing mindless activities such as watching calming television shows or reading for a while. When I watch familiar celebrities on television, like Jimmy Fallon or Seth Meyers, I feel as if I have a friend in my home and my stress level is reduced. At approximately 2:00 a.m. I am ready to go to bed - but first I need to check and recheck that all electrical appliances are shut off, the door is locked and my dog is safe and comfortable. My spine-chilling apprehensions make it difficult for me to feel safe because I imagine all of the calamities that could occur in the darkness. I fear that those that are closest to me may be harmed or that murderers and rapists are looming in my closets.

I am finally ready to share my bed with the bona fide monster lurking in my room, interminably breathing misery into my mind, body and soul. I close the light and slip under my covers, naked and vulnerable to the blacker, thicker dead of night which nature has specifically designated for deep sorrows and fears that have been obscured by the sun.

I try to find balance by reminding myself of all of my simple blessings, however I avoid succumbing to glorious fantasies of peace on earth, intimate relationships with lovers and friends, and children happily playing by my fireplace – because then I will awake to a new dawn casting shades of light on broken dreams.

Reflections on Chapter 16: Dawn to Dark

This chapter gives the broad term of depression a personal meaning by demonstrating how the symptoms of depression can take hold of each and every moment of a life, how every day rituals require tremendous physical and emotional effort, how feelings of isolation dominate the mind, and how the entire world is seen through dark-colored lenses.

It is important for those who care for someone who suffers from depression to understand the sheer despair in a day of the life of a depressive. Perhaps you will not be able to reverse all of the symptoms of depression but you can help a depressive evolve by understanding their affliction and reminding them of their self worth and personal strengths.

Chapter Seventeen

PSYCHOPHARMACEUTICALS

I was held captive by the prison of psychopharmaceuticals for over twenty years - but now I am free. The adverse side-effects from antidepressants contributed to the steady decline of my sense of self. I could not see the end to my emotional pain so I surrendered and all of my aspirations were laid to rest. Like an animal that instinctually faces death alone, I found a place to hide without human companionship as I suffered through the death of my spirit. As my peers were building careers and families, I remained in a drug-induced state of mind. One season followed another until the death of my spirit became my life story. My physical being survived, but the long term use of psychopharmaceuticals like Tricyclics, Monoamine Oxidase Inhibitors and Selective Serotonin Reuptake Inhibitors contributed to a lifetime of depression and physical pain. These chemicals sneakily feasted on my mind and body like greedy termites that move around undetected until their widespread destruction becomes irreparable. My only motivation was to try to find ways to suppress anxiety's demonic hold, but despite all of the mind-numbing drugs my anxiety persisted.

The conflict between emotion and reason always played a role when deciding whether to take antidepressants. I've heard it said that emotions are the enemy of reason, but it's my belief that sound decisions require a balanced relationship between emotions and reason. Looking back, I feel that the intense mixed emotions were there to warn me that I was destroying my life. Each time I started a new antidepressant I had hope for symptom relief while despairing that the outcome was beyond my control; I had courage to try a new course of drugs while fearing further emotional and physical pain. These contradictory emotions were inescapably woven together with each and every dose of solid flat tablets and multi-colored cylinder capsules.

Since my freedom from the bondage of psychopharmaceuticals I became more aware of the difficulty in finding mental health professionals who concentrate on holistic approaches for treatment of depression. Blank2 agrees with some of my feelings about these drugs, however in my earlier years of treatment with him the subject touched a nerve.

"One of the conditions of accepting you as my client is that you must see a psychiatrist for antidepressants," Blank2 said emphatically.

"I've experimented with antidepressants for years and I never experienced relief from my symptoms; in fact the drugs intensify my depression. I understand that many of your patients may feel differently, but I've wasted my life dulling my senses instead of dealing with my emotional pain and learning how to grow and change. My depression combined with all of the drugs caused me to withdraw from life instead of engage in it. Besides, I've become more and more sensitive to antidepressants and suffer excruciating adverse reactions, like akathesia, and I never want to go through those torturous symptoms again."

"There are many new drugs on the market that you haven't tried yet. I'd like you to see a psychiatrist to further evaluate your needs. As a psychologist I don't have prescribing privileges so this is not my area of expertise."

"Okay, I'll do it because I want to work with you but I don't trust psychiatrists anymore because their toxic chemicals never once, in two decades, alleviated my depression. The only relief I find is when I form a positive human connection and no drug in the world will bring me closer to loving relationships."

Since effective psychologists on Staten Island exist in fraying numbers I came to the conclusion that it was in my best interest to satisfy Blank2's ultimatum as well as my own need to find hope somewhere in the mental health system. Perhaps, I thought, one day Blank2 will come to respect me and we will experience greater equality in our decisions.

I decided to go to a Staten Island group that has access to the most recent advances in psychopharmacology. During my first consultation I agreed to become a volunteer patient for an antidepressant research trial. As an experimental subject I would have access to tests and the newest antidepressants on the market at no cost and I would be contributing to the advancement of the treatments for major depression. Although these seemed to be good reasons to start a new trial, I became increasingly apprehensive about starting the medication once I was home. The first few doses was always the most distressing as uncertainty played havoc on my psyche, but Blank2 had faith in the new drugs on the market and I had faith in Blank2.

My initial symptoms included an increase in anxious feelings, numbness in my lips and jaws and dizziness. As the week progressed I experienced language problems and retreated from conversations. When I found it too difficult to write I decided to cease taking the medication and since then I have not tried an antidepressant again. Writing had given me new aspirations and I was determined not to allow antidepressants to strip away my hope. There has always been a defining moment in the treatment process when I needed to decide whether the adverse side effects were acceptable.

As Blank2 witnessed some of my struggles with a new lens his feelings seemed to shift because he didn't bring up the subject of antidepressants for a long time. However, there came a time when my depression became intolerable and Blank2 suggested seeing a new psychiatrist to discuss antidepressants again and I agreed because the fear of living with the inward misery of depression was more terrifying than the fear of potential side effects. Blank2 was only comfortable recommending two prominent psychiatrists on Staten Island, Dr. L and Dr. K2. Since there appears to also be a shortage of good psychiatrists on Staten Island I had to wait about three months for my first appointment.

I finally met Dr. L on a wintery January evening in 2011. It was the beginning of a new year and I had a dim hope that I may be able to find a new beginning with greater peace of mind. Dr. L. had an authoritarian personality, rigid in his beliefs and opinions, and his appearance was similar to that of Sigmund Freud.

"Blank, your depression is too serious for me to treat. I also suspect that you are addicted to Xanax. I recommend an intensive outpatient hospital program so that you could be monitored closely."

At first I thought I misunderstood Dr. L.'s thick accent, but after a while I realized that I was being refused treatment unless I considered outpatient hospitalization. There was something about his authoritarian demeanor that gave me the feeling that he had power over my depression and I certainly needed someone to take control, however I would never willingly enter a psychiatric hospital again, even as an outpatient. In my despondency I humiliated myself by asking him to reconsider, but he felt too strongly about his conviction. Head held low, I walked away into the dark and cold night feeling the icy chill of hopelessness.

A few weeks later I went to see the second psychiatrist that Blank2 recommended. Dr. K2 was a middle aged woman with a nurturing personality and my immediate impression was that she was an experienced professional who would be committed to my medication needs. Dr. K2 asked questions about my history with depression, but even though I was guarded about the depth of my despondent feelings I observed that she was distressed.

"I see that you are extremely depressed. How do you manage to live with chronic depression?"

"I carry it with me every moment of the day in the same way that someone with a physical ailment learns to live with pain."

"I'm sorry Blank, but I am unable to take you on as a patient. Your depression has been resistant to treatment with antidepressants in the past. I could refer you to another psychiatrist off of Staten

Island who uses a controversial medication for treatment resistant patients."

"I know that I'm a difficult patient, but I didn't say that I was suicidal or unwilling to try another new antidepressant. Please reconsider because I'm unable to travel far for routine visits with another psychiatrist and, most importantly, Blank2 recommended you, so I have faith that you may be able to help me."

Once again I found myself pleading with a well-respected psychiatrist, but nonetheless she refused to treat me. The two rejections intensified my feelings of hopelessness and shame. I started to believe that I no longer deserved compassion or help from professionals because I'm too fallible. Why would a doctor want to treat someone who never exhibits symptom improvement, especially a difficult depressed patient like me? I discussed the rejection of the two psychiatrists with Blank2 upon my next session however I did not address my feelings of shame.

"I'm feeling more hopeless about my depression because both of the psychiatrists that you recommended refused to treat me. They believe I'm a difficult patient because my depression has been resistant to treatment. It's ironic and almost funny that I'm literally too depressed to be treated by well-respected psychiatrists, even though they are the very physicians who specialize in mood disorders."

"I'm not giving up on you," Blank2 said compassionately. "There are times when I'm ashamed of the mental health system."

Finally Blank2 was walking beside me and witnessing my journey. Instead of looking through the limits of books and journals he looked directly into my eyes and understood the limitless struggles of a depressive attempting to navigate the mental health system alone. The gift of validation from an expert in the field of psychology empowered me to move forward. I began to do my own research into the precarious world of psychopharmaceuticals and what I discovered is astounding: There is no cure for depression and scientific research is not progressing.

Antidepressants are believed to balance some of the chemicals in the brain called neurotransmitters which affect mood - however this has never been proven. There is a popular notion that depression can be alleviated by correcting serotonin deficiencies – however this has never been proven. The fact is that researchers know very little about how antidepressants work and the effectiveness of antidepressants has never been proven to work better than placebos - except placebos are innocuous while antidepressants are chemicals with potential adverse side effects.

All those years of erroneous information have been revealed to me. It's tragic that there are countless people, like me, whose lives have been destroyed because of these mind altering drugs. The continual use of antidepressants has been more disabling than my depression and I live in fear as I think about the unknown long-term damages to my brain.

Furthermore, pharmaceutical companies and funders have nearly deserted their efforts to advance research. One of the reasons there is a lack of funding is that there is less known about mental disorders than diseases like cancer, so research would take much longer and become too expensive; and the other hindrance is that there is still stigma surrounding depression and other mental disorders so there is less philanthropic efforts than when compared to other diseases.

The days when I see myself and everything around me through a distorted lens, when my depressed emotions are so obscure and insufferable that I am unable to describe the feelings using our expansive lexicon - it is especially daunting to know that I stand alone in a mental battlefield because medical science is unable to help me today and is making very little progress for tomorrow. It is my impassioned hope and plea that science will find a way to further explore the underlying causes of depression because perhaps then we can find a cure one day.

There is, however, something significant and meaningful that we could do to help today: Those affected by chronic depression and their families and friends can speak openly about the mood disorder so that we could increase awareness of mental illness and the need for compassion and funding. Individuals with mental illness live with a sense of disgrace because of all of the popular misconceptions about their disease. If we are courageous enough to reveal our truth – we can begin the process of change.

Given all of my adverse side effects from antidepressants through two decades some may wonder why I considered psychopharmaceuticals for treatment of my depression over and over again, so let me explain. At the onset, I wasn't aware of the controversies surrounding psychopharmaceuticals. I trusted that the pharmaceutical companies had scientifically proven safe and effective drugs that would help diminish my symptoms of depression and I also trusted the opinions of the psychiatrists who prescribed the drugs. In addition, whenever I endured agonizing symptoms I was left with two options: surrender to depression or seek help in all the resources that were available despite all of the horrendous side-effects.

The decision to take antidepressants is a serious one and requires careful consideration. Depression hurts, as the popular antidepressant commercial states, but sometimes despairing emotions are necessary and can be a catalyst for growth. When symptoms become too unmanageable seek help from a therapist. An effective therapist can help without the adverse life altering side-effects of antidepressants. Perhaps therapists are unable to cure chronic depression but they have the skills to help you to see problems from a new perspective and to make choices that could improve the quality of your life. The ability to discuss your thoughts and feelings with a learned and compassionate listener is extremely healing.

So, yes, I am at long last walking away from the prison of psychopharmaceuticals after relinquishing over twenty years of my life – and you will be surprised to know how I gained my freedom. My freedom does not come from continually blaming psychiatrists and pharmaceutical companies for my long-term captivity. Instead, it comes from finally taking some personal responsibility and action for the treatment of my depression. My years of experience and research have empowered me to make informed decisions on psychopharmaceuticals and in this knowledge I have found freedom. I now feel a strong drive to help other depressives who are making treatment decisions - giving meaning to what once seemed like meaningless pain.

Reflections of Chapter 17: Psychopharmaceuticals

As I reflected on this chapter I was grateful that I found freedom in taking some responsibility for the treatment of my depression. I am also grateful for the gift of finding meaning in my pain.

As a result of my lifetime issues with depression I am occasionally asked to render advice on treatments for depression. The most frustrating aspect for me is addressing the idealized relationship between psychopharmaceuticals and depression. Over and over again individuals believe that a pill could cure depression, a simplistic assumption most likely arrived at because of direct consumer marketing. My response is to enlighten caregivers and sufferers of some of the uncertainties of antidepressants and to remind them of the importance of doing their own research before making a decision - because I do not want anyone to suffer my fate.

ACCEPTANCE

Chapter Eighteen

AHA MOMENT

A few years ago I experienced a moment of clarity, a moment when my past burdens became a gift. It all happened when I visited my relative who was struggling for days in a relentless, agitated state of inconsolable grief. Amid her disorientation and frantic howls that seemed to emerge from deep within, I offered her comfort with an open, loving heart. Finally, her hollow eyes became fixed on mine as she rested her head on my shoulder and wearily surrendered her raw emotional pain. There was sheer power in her silent surrender that echoed from wall to wall and beyond the physical dimensions of the room. In that moment I understood that my incomprehensible past propelled me to a place where I could make a tender connection with another human being - and that my struggles had a purpose.

The roots of my transformative moment began with an old story of a fabulous foursome which I have preserved in my heart's treasure chest. My parents and their two cousins and lifetime friends, Eva and Nate, were the epitome of the last generation of innocence of the late 1940's and 1950's. When Eva and Nate and my mother and father were together life was in balance, whole and as complete as the four seasons and the four corners of the earth.

The story, according to the version told by Eva, goes like this:

My mother and Eva attended a community dance in Brooklyn, New York in the 1950's to enjoy a little dancing and meet nice fellows. My father bashfully introduced himself to my mother but she expressed disinterest. My father was an apprehensive man and wasn't comfortable around girls, especially attractive girls, so he walked away feeling defeated.

"Millie, why don't you talk with that charming man? He has a beautiful smile and nice thick black hair. Go find him and let him know you're interested," Eva cajoled.

"But he's so shy and not at all a dapper dresser and he probably drives an old jalopy."

My mother and father were very opposite in disposition. My mother was an extrovert who was energized in social situations. She had a keen ability to talk with just about anyone on the street or in a crowded room. Although my mother's values were old fashioned she was not like the typical young woman of her time who were concerned with learning how to cook, clean and do laundry. Instead my mother had an obsessive interest in glamorous trends like the new haute couture fashions.

My father was reserved and yet he possessed the wonderful trait of being able to express his sense of humor. Dad had an insatiable passion for music, especially the big band and swing era. He loved the sounds of artists like Artie Shaw, Glenn Miller, Tommy Dorsey and Benny Goodman.

Eventually my mother took Eva's advice and asked my father to dance. Although my father was a shy gentleman his passion for music compelled him to step outside of his comfort zone and dance the night away. My father seemed to believe that life isn't sweet unless you incorporate a little swing, like Duke Ellington's classic jazz piece, "It Don't Mean a Thing, If It Ain't Got That Swing."

Mom and Dad and Eva and Nate began keeping company, as was the expression of that generation, and they fell in love. The two couples were wholesome people who exerted exuberance for life and all of its possibilities. My father and Nate were from a generation of men that didn't have a great deal of money and Dutch Dating was unheard of back then so they frequented places that were affordable and fun like the local dances. No matter what they did they had a blast when they were together. Eventually things progressed into the customary going steady and then a proposal.

My parents never discussed intimacy, but years later Eva confided in me that Papa Peter, my grandfather, caught mom and dad "necking" by the curbside. Papa Peter seldom spoke but his strong demeanor was still feared by family and even his community. Rumor has it that my grandfather was considered a Consigliore which is a counselor and confidant to the boss of the American Mafia. It's comforting for me to assume that the rumor is a fallacy since it is incongruent with my grandparents' modest lifestyle and their values.

Eva went on to say that when my parents realized they were caught by Papa Peter my mother told my father to run. So dad jumped over the bushes and ran through the streets of Brooklyn all the way home. It's a cowardly act indeed however my father's strength would become apparent as the years progressed. During their courtship my mother began to show symptoms of her illness and Papa Peter and Grandma Cristina told my father that they would understand if he chose to walk away from his impending marriage to their daughter. My father informed my mother and her family that he was committed to loving my mother regardless of her illness.

The rest of the story became part of my own personal history. My mother's chronic illness progressed through the years and Eva and Nate faithfully stood by and continued their weekly visits until my mother was moved to a nursing facility. It was quite an amazing friendship considering that most people disappeared from my parents' lives, unable to cope with the trauma related to a debilitating illness. My mother's illness not only encompassed the loss of physical health, but the loss of self as friends and family began to drift away. However despite my mother's decline the couples' friendship was strengthened by love and laughter, plenty of laughter.

Eva and Nate came from their Brooklyn home to visit my parents in Staten Island almost every Saturday evening from my adolescence through young adulthood. Oftentimes I would pick-up a video from the local video rental shop for the couples to watch, however it was difficult for them to view the movie without incessant interruptions. My mother and Nate were avid conversationalists with a wide range of interests, even when my mother's voice had become weakened by her disease, and during the movie my mother and Nate would converse about family and current issues in the news. My father and Eva would roll their eyes and try to ignore them but when they could no longer tolerate the raucous they would be straightforward and express their frustrations, however their candor was only met with contagious laughter.

Eva and Nate added a sense of normalcy to my parents' lives and my heart will be forever thankful to them. It's been many years since those days and sorrowfully my parents and Eva and Nate are all deceased. Eva was the last of the fabulous four to take her final breath in January 2013. She was doing reasonably well until her young son passed away from complications of heart disease a couple of years earlier. Eva began to display signs of Alzheimer's the previous year and the death of her son sent her spiraling into the darkness of the disease in a matter of days. I speculate that her sudden decline was her minds way of protecting itself from her tragic loss.

Eva began calling me days after the loss of her son and her conversations would drift from the past to the present. I decided to visit Eva in her Brooklyn home so that I could reciprocate the kindness that she had shown to my parents for so many years. Eva's home was just as I remembered as a child with traditional paintings, family photographs and a large formal dining room table which at one time accommodated three generations of family including my late grandmother and her sisters. I was honored to see that Eva prominently displayed my mother's porcelain blue birds, a token that I had given Eva after my mother's death. What struck me the most was that her brooding home appeared void and empty - as if love and laughter had remained unreplenished far too long.

The death of Eva's son was an inconceivable loss however Eva's emotional world became depleted through many years of losses. It's the unreplenishment of things that destroy our soul and result in illnesses like dementia for the elderly and persistent depression for individuals like myself. I am certain that it was not one incident that caused my long-term battles with depression but many years of heartaches that were not accompanied with new experiences and new joy.

When I saw Eva she was gasping for air and screaming, a kind of primal scream, as she paced from room to room. It was a similar scream to the one I heard not too long ago from a woman in Macy's at the Staten Island Mall, a scream that unmistakably reveals a sudden tragic event. The woman in Macy's had plenty of support so I walked away however I was feeling shaken and concerned about the nature of her pain. Later that evening I spoke with my brother and discussed the scenario that I had witnessed in the department store.

"Why do you always assume the worse," my brother asked in frustration. "Maybe she was screaming because she just found out that she won the lottery. Just forget about it."

"Lou, I recognize that kind of scream and without a doubt something tragic just occurred in that woman's life. I feel terribly sad for her."

How could I just forget about the woman's heartache? My very being has been formed by emotional anguish and I've spent a lifetime contemplating on my own sadness and the sadness of the people around me.

However, unlike the woman in the mall, Eva's screams would not cease in intensity. Eva's daughter, Deana, was distraught because she had just lost her only sibling and was also trying to cope with her mother's sudden decline. Deana compassionately cared for her mother however at the moment of my visit she needed a brief respite.

As the nurse's aide prepared Eva's medication I asked to be allowed some time alone with her so that I could try a non-pharmaceutical approach. I'm typically a touch avoidant person but I somehow innately knew that Eva needed a compassionate touch. So I took Eva's hand and we sat on the sofa and I began my personal form of touch and compassion therapy.

"You know I care about you. Imagine my love running through your hands and up through the veins in your arms and then finally filling your heart," I said softly while gently touching her hands, arms and heart. Can you do that Eva?"

I repeated these unadorned words until Eva placed her head on my shoulders, slipped her legs across the sofa, and finally rested. It seemed I had reached Eva's rudimentary sense of being comforted. I continued to express my love and gratitude to her because the one thing that I know for certain is that love is the ultimate elixir for almost everything.

"Your mother is less agitated," the nurse's aide said to Deana.

"Blank has had problems with depression and anxiety for many years so she understands how to help," Deana explained.

And directly after hearing Deana's words I experienced my vital aha moment of clarity. Until that time I didn't consciously realize that my past enabled me to serve others in despair and this new awareness brought extraordinary meaning into my life. I had the innate ability to effectively comfort Eva because I have experienced an enduring pattern of suffering. I understood that Eva's primal howls were the only capacity that she had left to purge her grief; and I understood that my simple methods of expressing empathy would help Eva in her time of deep anguish. I knew this because - I have been there.

My inner demons prevented me from seeing that I had the capacity to help people in despair - and the love that I offered Eva expelled the darkness and allowed me to see the light, as if it were a spiritual exorcism. Yet, it is of vital importance to note, I could not have been set free from my sense of emptiness until I experienced utter starvation. As I began to readjust the way that I thought about my past I realized that all my losses, sickness, humiliation and abandonment were in a sense gifts waiting to give birth to compassion and wisdom. This knowledge has changed the way I think of the meaninglessness of my struggles.

Although I knew the narrative of the fabulous four for decades the progression of time changed its meaning because I, the observer of their story, continue to grow and change. The final chapter of a beautiful story of friendship has sadly come to an end however a new chapter of hope has begun as I seek opportunities to find greater meaning in my struggles.

Reflections on Chapter 18: Aha Moment

Through the years I have felt as if my life has fallen into an abyss of meaninglessness because of my depressive illness. This chapter demonstrates how a meaningful encounter could whisper to our spirit to try just one more time. My innate ability to help a beloved relative made it easier for me to begin to conceptualize a life of greater meaning. As a result of my experience with Eva and analogous encounters I began writing my book and I began to dream about a future as a helping professional.

It takes courage to bring about meaningful life changes, especially for depressives who are struggling with debilitating emotions, but it's worth the effort because the glorious outcome will be a more positive outlook on life. What helped me to find meaning was to observe the subject matters that I enjoyed learning about and sharing with others, those subjects where I felt a soulful engagement and most at peace with myself. Once I found what brought about feelings of harmony I attempted to structure my life in a way that incorporated those things where I feel a sense of passion.

Chapter Nineteen

BLIND SPOTS

A shadowy curtain descended over my vision as I was writing the final chapters of my book in the summer of 2014. Ironically as my life was becoming more visible through the writing journey I was experiencing a physical visual deficit. I did not consider the blurriness to be a medical emergency because weeks before my symptoms surfaced I had a routine comprehensive eye exam and received a clean bill of health. As the weeks progressed I was becoming increasingly anxious about my visual limitations, but going back to the Ophthalmologist also caused a sense of unease. Oftentimes my anxiety disorder prevents me from seeking medical care because I literally feel imprisoned by my fears.

A fortuitous encounter at a business event with C. W., an Optician, changed the course of my visual health when he discovered that I had a detached retina. At that time I was working part-time for the non-profit organization for ten years and the stress of the office work and their large-scale events had become ordinary, however this encounter was a stark reminder of everyday miracles. The reality that I maintained a job for ten years with my chronic emotional problems is a phenomenon; the occurrence of an Optician expressing a sincere interest in my well-being at precisely that moment was extraordinary. I observe the world through dark colored-lenses, habitually too blind to see the light in everyday life. This experience allowed me to see my physical and psychological blind spots with greater clarity.

C.W. referred me to a local retinal specialist, a highly trained medical doctor who specializes in diseases of the retina and retina surgery. I learned that the retina is the light sensitive tissue in the back of the eye which sends visual messages to the brain and that blurred vision will occur if the retina becomes separated from its normal position. Permanent blindness occurs if the retinal detachment is not immediately treated. I was fully awake when the retinal specialist began the procedure and respectfully informed me that my case was beyond his expertise. I was then referred to the New York Eye and Ear Infirmary in Manhattan as an emergency. It was at this point that my fears and apprehensions went haywire as I pondered the possibility of blindness in the affected eye.

My brother accompanied me to the New York Eye and Ear Infirmary and offered support throughout the ordeal. All morning my eyes were examined by countless ophthalmologists who used unbearable beams of light and probes to see the back of the eye until I literally could take no more and burst into tears. The experience was not painful, but what affected me the most were the duration of the tests and the inability of the physicians to treat me as a whole person. I was thankful that they were trying to help and never believed they were callous, I simply felt that they did not understand the power of empathy. I wish that I could have reminded them that I am more than a cornea, iris and retina; I am a human being with eyes that have grown weary from sadness - and - with eyes that widen with the beauty of snow-covered landscapes. And, for similar reasons, I wish that I could remind mental health providers that I am more than the neurotransmitters in my brain; I am a human being who experiences anxiety and depression and, yes, sometimes even joy and hopefulness.

By midafternoon Dr. J. L. and the attending surgeon, Dr. K. L., took control of my case, both imparting an air of understanding and knowledge and my fears were subdued. They carefully evaluated my situation and decided that immediate surgery was necessary. Apprehensively, I told Dr. K. L. about my anxiety disorder and he was receptive, providing valuable information on various types of anesthesia and, most importantly, empathy. As thankful as I was that he was helping me, I was wishing he also could offer a surgical procedure that would repair the flaws in my brain.

I was told that I would be in surgery in about one hour, but time took upon a warped meaning for me that day so the entire perception of an hour shifted into some unknown measurement. The past twenty-four hours seemed to be going by in slow motion, as often happens to me when I'm going through a life-changing event.

Finally I walked into the surgical room and was given twilight anesthesia, a mild dose of drugs which provide temporary memory loss and block pain and anxiety. Despite the twilight anesthesia, I recall the blood pressure monitor cuff on my upper arm slowly loosening and tightening its grip, imagining that each squeeze of the cuff was a comforting hug from another human being - and I didn't want the exquisite feeling to come to an end. The next thing I remember is Dr. K. L. bringing me back to conscious awareness and my drug-induced state of peacefulness slowly coming to an end. I had bandages across both eyes so I could not see anyone in the room but was aware that there was a team of people. My first words expressed my deep gratitude to each of them for helping me gain back the precious gift of sight.

During the surgery my affected eye was filled with long-acting gas bubbles to prevent a new retinal detachment. I was instructed to remain completely face-down for the next three weeks so that the gas bubbles would float to the detachment and remain there until a seal is formed between the retina and the wall of the eye. Not remaining face-down, including sleeping, walking, resting and eating, would possibly result in another retinal detachment, glaucoma, accelerate the growth of cataracts, and damage the cornea. The gas bubbles cause temporary blindness in the affected eye but as they gradually diffuse and natural fluids fill the space the vision is expected to improve.

This is not a passive healing process and given the grave consequences of not staying face-down, it behooved me to heed the advice of my surgeons. I had to quickly develop a way to cope as I resumed the face-down position for what turned out to be almost 60 days. The first month I was in the face-down position all of the time, except for the dispensing of eye drops, and the next month I was in the face-down position for approximately 70% of the day. Predictably, the face-down position had a damaging affect on my depression. There seems to be a correlation between the brain and body posture because I can attest that walking around with a crestfallen posture contributes to depression.

As a person who lives alone my sense of isolation was very real and I felt detached from the emotional care that I needed; and all of my routine activities, like cleaning, cooking, writing and my quality of sleep were grossly interrupted. There are devices to help with face-down recovery, but I wasn't feeling strong enough to research equipment and to attempt to attain the necessary approvals from my insurance company. As the days progressed I realized that I was feeding my depression and anxiety with negative thoughts, allowing my symptoms to persist and even flourish. The loss of vision in the affected eye caused a profound decrease in my overall visual acuity. I learned that people can see significantly better with both eyes working together than by either of the eyes functioning alone. As far back as I could remember I have had a deep appreciation for my sense of sight, taking the time each day to observe the view from my apartment window and the symmetry of a genuine smile, so the fear of being visually impaired was overwhelming. In addition to the fear of losing the ability to see the beauty in everyday life I was consumed with fear of losing my independence and also fear of not being able to finish my book. When I am most isolated and frightened it seems that all I have left are my negative thoughts.

As the weeks and months progressed I experienced numerous complications and my vision was not improving within the expected recovery period. Since I was directly responsible for my recovery I assumed that I had done something wrong, that I looked up too many times during the day, that I did not administer my eye drops correctly, that I sneezed or coughed too hard, or that once again I was remiss in taking care of my own well-being. I was unable to return to work and the financial strain and loss of independence was becoming more and more daunting with each passing day. Studies demonstrate that visual impairment is directly linked with anxiety and depression so it only stands to reason that I would be prone to profound feelings of hopelessness.

One afternoon an Ophthalmologist at the Infirmary said those most dreaded words during recovery: "There is nothing more we can do for you." I was devastated and I requested that Dr. K. L. come in to confirm these findings. About an hour later Dr. K. L. walked into the exam room and offered hope. I then became a private patient of Dr. K. L. and my exams took place in his office outside of the Infirmary which was more physically and emotionally comfortable. This change improved the quality of our communication and our physician-patient relationship. As a result, I developed more faith in my treatment plan. In addition, my brother's willingness to accompany me to Dr. K. L.'s downtown Manhattan office routinely and Blank2's telephone calls of support had a profound effect on my recovery.

My visual impairment paved the way to unlikely comparisons. At a certain point in my recovery I oddly appreciated some aspects of my visual problems when I compared them to my depressive illness. I was particularly grateful that I was not completely blindsided by the onset of my detached retina and that there were viable treatment plans; whereas my depression took on a colorless beginning and I can't see an end to the pain. Also, since my detached retina didn't cause extreme physical pain I was able to divert my attention during my recovery; whereas my depression is an all-consuming misery without periods of rest. And, my detached retina was something that I didn't need to hide because people understood the physical, some were even sympathetic; whereas depression has become a secret sorrow because of long-held stigmas. Dealing with an illness in a supportive environment makes a world of difference.

In time I found additional ways to lift my spirits, like reading from my electronic reader where I could adjust the visual settings, a visit from an angel in my life, M. D., and observing my short-legged dog who was always in my visual space. I began to see things from a more positive perspective, most likely because I held onto hope that things would improve. Implausibly, I even began to appreciate the introspective beauty of looking at the world through a serene shadowy curtain. More and more I realized that despite my depression I have a true appreciation for life and its physical loveliness.

Seven months later I was heading to Dr. K. L.'s office during the snowstorm of March 2015 one day after my second eye surgery. I recall the feeling of exhilaration when Dr. K. L. removed my bandages and I began testing my improved vision in his dark exam room, but nothing could have prepared me for the moment that I stepped out of his office and into a winter wonderland. Even with my dark post-operative sun glasses, I was able to see the snow and ice glistening, like shattered pieces of elegant crystal, on the narrow streets of Tribeca with full-blown clarity and glaring brightness. I stretched out my hands and allowed the snowflakes to fall onto my mittens while whispering the words, "thank you."

I still have visual complications but I am incredibly thankful for how far I have come in my recovery. It's been over a year since my surgeries and Dr. K. L. indicated that my eye has healed beautifully, but I will need to see him indefinitely because my eye will always be sensitive and vulnerable. The thought of more complications is daunting, but I'm definitely ready to move forward with my life. I am now embracing the lessons that I have learned through my visual impairment and I'm grateful that I have an opportunity to bring awareness of the psychological challenges of visual impairment, eye surgery, and face-down recovery through my book.

Mostly, I feel grateful that at the end of one of my longest nights - I am seeing the light – with a renewed appreciation for the visual beauty that is all around me.

Reflections of Chapter 19: Blind Spots

While reviewing this chapter it occurred to me that despite my chronic battles with depression and suicidal ideation, I have a deep appreciation for life. I appreciate the perpetual blessings of new insights gained whenever my mental blind spots are revealed, and, I appreciate the miraculous gift of the sense of sight.

It is important that those who suffer from depression and those who care for them understand that chronic depression is a disease that is persistent regardless of feelings of gratitude. However, gratitude absolutely serves as a buffer to profound feelings of sadness in the present and it's a starting point to dream and hope for a better tomorrow. It's of vital importance, whether or not we are depressed, to take time to acknowledge the gift of every breath we take as well as human generosity and the wondrous landscapes that sustains us.

Chapter Twenty

GOODBYE

It's difficult to say goodbye but nonetheless it is my time to create a new destiny. I am grieving my loss as the final curtain is lowered on the writing of this book and my connection to you and the cherished people and places of my past. Years of heightened observation deepened my awareness of self and evoked a renewed affection toward the important people and places in my life as the true nature of things began to be revealed.

This shift in feelings and awareness cemented my intentions of honoring my past and staying connected to individuals who are struggling with depression and anxiety once my book is complete. Over the last few years I have found a voice as I penned the darkness of a depressive disorder and I resolve not to go back to silence and apathy once the ink is dry. Each day I become stronger as I purge my personal narrative and lift the weight of shame and silence. I am finally taking a proactive role in becoming the person that I would like to be - and I want to positively influence others to manage adversity and discover their inner strength.

In 2015, I accepted a position at a hospital in Staten Island as an assistant to an Administrative Director who manages out-patient clinics and various physician practices that operate under the umbrella of the hospital. Even though the transitional period would throw me entirely off-balance I faced my fears and apprehensions head-on because I believed that a fresh start would be good for me and I hoped that the hospital environment would bring me closer to the service of others.

Tendering my resignation to C.C., the President of the small local non-profit organization where I was employed for eleven years, was distressing. I thought of many of my coworkers as my family, especially during those times when we worked as a team toward a goal, supported one another through difficulties and celebrated milestones.

I was deeply humbled and almost equally surprised when the organization planned a resignation dinner in my honor. Approximately twenty of my coworkers and even former coworkers attended as well as C.C. and S.F., a member of the Executive Board of Directors. A transformative moment occurred when each of the attendees imparted a testimonial about my character. I was especially touched by those who thanked me for the small ways that I supported them through difficult challenges because although contributing to the organization's mission was important to me - helping others was my ultimate intention.

After everyone spoke I found myself gazing out the window with tearful eyes, observing the brightly colored sun setting on a slice of suburbia in the south shore of Staten Island. I was able to live in the moment of this spectacular night, enjoying the surroundings through my entire range of senses. Privately, my resignation dinner represented triumph over adversity since my success is less about achievement and more about the difficult journey. Praise always contradicts the image that I have of myself but on this night I rose above my self-doubt because I was accepting the accolades on behalf of all my kindred spirits who suffer from psychological disorders and try, despite all odds, to reach their potential.

As I started to become fully immersed in my new responsibilities at the hospital, a deep sadness was smoldering every aspect of my day and my hopefulness was steadily dwindling. This is an example of what depression does to its victims. It snuffs out the fire of your hopes and dreams and reduces them to ashes over and over again. Sometimes it seems that my depressive symptoms are a by-product of my unrealistic hope.

"I'm having difficulty adjusting to my job," I lamented to Blank2. "I took a step backward in my career in order to pursue goals that I'm more passionate about. I was told that since it's a new position at the hospital my responsibilities would be established over time, but to expect that sometimes I would be given quality work and sometimes not. It turns out that I'm working almost exclusively on billing and payroll and I'm functioning poorly because I don't have this type of background and I'm losing confidence. It doesn't look like I'll ever be given assignments that will be in alignment with some of my goals and dreams. And - there's something else."

"What is it?"

"Well, I'm wondering if I may never be able to experience happiness again. It's far too late in my life to attain the things that would make me most happy like a meaningful career, children and grandchildren. The times when I feel most at peace are when I'm in a position to help someone who's hurting, like when my friend lost her husband far too soon, or when an acquaintance needed advice on her depression and medication therapy. It's only in those fleeting moments that I feel that I finally found my way back home. I may have discovered more about myself and my passion over the last few years but that has not brought me closer to my goals."

"Blank, you live in the past. It may be too late to achieve certain goals, but every day is a chance to start over again and explore things that would help you to feel better. Why don't you consider becoming certified as a Life Coach?"

"I don't know what you're talking about."

"A Life Coach uses skills and techniques that help people achieve personal goals and build the kind of lives that they've always wanted. You can even coach people living with depression and anxiety. I'm recommending this to you because I believe that you already have the ability to be a good listener and I feel that you can really help people."

"It's probably too costly to become credentialed and it's definitely far too late in my life."

"It may be affordable and you could become a Life Coach within a year. You even have the option to take online classes."

I needed a few minutes to digest what Blank2 was proposing. I never before put the words "life" and "coach" together and when I did it seemed to be life changing. After dreaming about a gratifying profession for so many years I could hardly believe that it may be possible, especially with all of the constraints of my depressive illness. I knew that there must be impassable roadblocks so I tried to stop ruminating on the possibility, but my hopes and fears were rapidly firing questions at me as if I were a shooting target. Suddenly, Blank2's voice broke my deep introspection.

"Why aren't you saying something? I'll take your silence to mean that you're considering my great suggestion. I don't want to tell you what to do but I think this may be something worthwhile to pursue."

Blank2 often says that he doesn't want to tell me what to do, but this time I needed him to shout from the highest mountain because he believes wholeheartedly that I am worth it and because he truly believes that becoming a Life Coach has the potential to change the trajectory of my life. I needed him to assert his courage, hope and commitment because I could not find those things in myself.

I glanced at the clock across the room and realized that it was getting late. One of the problems in therapy is that once you are comfortable enough to expand on your feelings - your time has expired. I slowly walked to my car under a full moon on a dark chilly night while my sinister lone shadow beckoned me, as if to remind me of my fate. The thought that I may never find fulfillment and lasting happiness occupied my mind.

It's been many years since I stood at the edge of a railing on the Golden Gate Bridge and today thoughts of suicide continue to ravage my mind, but I'm committed to stifling those thoughts and feelings. The accumulation of all of my losses and heightened sense of loneliness since that day has augmented my sadness a hundredfold.

Some survivors of a suicide attempt or suicidal ideation eventually discover healing and hope but what sustains individuals, like me, who struggle with chronic depressive disorders and live the remainder of their lives with an enveloping sense of emotional pain?

What sustained me at times was the fight to find hope in my future self, but my advanced age has forced me to look at life with a different intent because I now possess a profound understanding of the limits of time. Middle adulthood is a frightening phase in a person's life, especially for those who have been unable to find a sense of purpose and belonging. What the young don't understand is that many older adults feel as if they are young and vibrant people mysteriously trapped in an ageing person's body. My aspirations are the same as when I was in my twenties however I feel as if I travelled forward in time at the speed of light and landed in the autumn of my life with all of its nasty limitations. The fact that I wasted precious years battling my depression seems like an unacceptable violation to my humanity. When I look in the mirror I am shocked to see signs of ageing. The only silver lining of finding silvery strands in my hair is that it is a reminder that life is a brief journey and it's time to do much more than sit around and passively find hope in my future self. It's time to contribute to the world and shine. It's time to take massive action!

As I thought about the meaning of my life since my last session with Blank2 I had an emotional breakthrough: I need to accept that depression will forever breathe within my soul. If I want to have a more fulfilling life I must discover unfaltering methods of integrating acceptance, passion and human connection into a life that is compromised by depression. This notion of acceptance is simple and yet it is perhaps my greatest personal discovery. It's stupefying how acceptance remains elusive until a person comes to the end of a long and winding road, exhausted and desperate.

Life for everyone is imperfect but we must summon up the courage to accept our afflictions in order to become our greatest selves. I'm not purporting that it's possible to totally ignore whatever it is that brings us pain, but as an alternative we must accept adversity and learn to live alongside of it with peace of mind. Instead of using all of our energy fighting the pain, we could challenge ourselves and allot some of that energy to finding ways to establish goals that may lead us to a more hopeful tomorrow.

At a certain time in all of our lives we must discover ways to comfortably live with our inner darkness – because paradoxically it is the only way we will find the light. There is a time for sorrow and a time when we must look for the dim light that assuredly shines in the darkness. It is our responsibility to live fully - despite adversity. For many of us adversity is a constant part of our life, not a temporary state of being, and we are left with two options: suffer the death of our soul or dare to discover the special beauty that lives in sorrow. I chose the latter with a decision that sets me free from some of the restrictions of a depressive illness.

In early 2016, I graduated from a prominent training program that is accredited by the International Coaching Federation and I became a certified Life Coach. One year later I received a second certification as a Wellness Coaching Specialist, a specialized area of coaching that entails a holistic approach which integrates the mind, body and spirit. I completed the rigorous requirements for both certifications more quickly than I could have ever imagined because I was starving for a new life and a platform to help other depressives who are ready to move forward.

My coaching practice emphasizes empathetic listening and the encouragement of hope, motivation and action. Unfortunately finding hope and motivation is a challenge for many of us, especially depressives, however the life coaching process is enormously effective in helping people find the motivation to live life more fully - one small step at a time. I encourage my clients to honor their lives by not passively surrendering to the countless obstacles that come their way. Hope is not meant to be a passive concept. Hope is a verb that requires purposeful action in order to elicit change. I am here to attest that with the support of a skilled accountability partner – change and transformation is possible.

My depressive illness swapped the colors of a yellowy day and catapulted me into an alternate universe where the world is a surreal colorless grey. But even in my monochrome dimension, hanging on the precipice of despair, I am grateful to be alive. Since the success of my eye surgeries not long ago, I have learned to keep my eyes wide open because they will too soon be forever closed and I already lost far too much time. In my daily routines I am deeply aware of the exquisiteness of the gentle rhythm of the wind and the beauty that is all around me and I am thankful for those precious, colorful moments when my depressive lens is lifted.

And, before the final curtain has fallen, I want to say to my kindred spirits who struggle with depression - that I care about you and you are not alone in your darkness. I say goodbye to you in this limited format - but the energy of compassion and connectedness that the writing of this book has inspired is as infinite and expansive as the starry sky above us.

Reflections on Chapter 20: Goodbye

This chapter asks a vital question: Can chronically depressed individuals find happiness? I'm not certain if happiness is possible for depressives, but I do know in my heart that when individuals who are predisposed to depression find greater meaning in their lives - positive emotions can be accessed.

The problem for depressives is that we lack the energy and motivation to discover those things that may bring greater meaning to our lives. However, sometimes the pain of depression itself can motivate us to help others who are also tottering on the precipice of the dark abyss. The ability to help others is powerfully meaningful.

My own struggles have helped me to evolve as I discovered the gift of wisdom that is a byproduct of depression. I often feel irritated by the familiar sentiments on how adversity helps us to evolve, but at the same time, I know that my struggles were the catalyst for writing my book and becoming a Life Coach. My depression was not the beautifully wrapped gift that I wished for when I speculated on my future as a youth. It has instead been an unwanted and painful offering in which, on a good day, I can transform into something meaningful.

I want depressives to know the importance of finding a life with greater meaning. Once you find what it is that brings meaning to your life you will be able to tap into energy that you never knew existed. A life with greater meaning will at the very least fill some of the emptiness that is intrinsic to the depressive illness. Each small step that you take today will lead to a more purposeful and hopeful tomorrow. Hope is a verb.

www.ingramcontent.com/pod-product-compliance
Lightning Source LLC
Chambersburg PA
CBHW071334280526
45787CB00001B/92